KILL·ALL·THE·JUDGES

DAVID CROSS

an
ABC
BOOK

Other humour by the author:

Books
I'll Plead Insanity
George and the Widda-Woman
The Mug Gardener's Handbook

Plays
Patsy for Parliament
Happy the Bride

Published by ABC Enterprises for the
AUSTRALIAN BROADCASTING CORPORATION
20 Atchison Street (Box 8888) Crows Nest NSW 2065

First published 1985
Reprinted 1985
This edition published February 1990

National Library of Australia
Cataloguing-in-Publication entry
Cross, David.
Kill all the judges.
ISBN 0 7333 0025 1.
I. Title.
A823.3

Text illustrations by George Luke
Cover designed by Jerome Gask
Set by Midland Typesetters, Victoria

TEXT ILLUSTRATIONS BY GEORGE LUKE

Any resemblance between the characters and events in this book and any person living or dead or any occurrence past present or future would not only be fortuitous and completely unintentional, but also quite incredible.

ACKNOWLEDGEMENT

The trial of The Attractive Young Widow v. The Commissioner of Probate Duties was inspired by an article in PUNCH written by A. P. Herbert and appears by kind permission of the Publishers of PUNCH and the Executors of the Estate of the late Sir Alan Herbert.

CONTENTS

The first thing we do, let's kill all the lawyers.

- William Shakespeare
(King Henry VI, Part 2, Act IV, Scene ii, line 86)

LOCKED IN A LAVATORY

I was in full flight of oratory, endeavouring to bedazzle a very grim-looking jury with my voluble flow of eloquence, when from on high the presiding trial judge suddenly interrupted. 'No doubt her husband had his defects,' the Honourable Mr. Justice Broote grumped, 'but these were not to be remedied by giving him doses of disinfectant.'

This priceless pearl of judicial wisdom was shattered by a shrill voice from the dock. 'I wasn't there,' the Accused wife cried out, 'and if I was I didn't do it.'

'There you are, Y'r Honour,' I exclaimed hastily and triumphantly, 'my client is innocent. She admits it herself.'

'I am innocent,' the Accused echoed, making the most of a good thing, 'Innocent, innocent!'

'You ain't,' screeched her mother-in-law from the public gallery.

The learned judge scowled savagely around the courtroom to quell any further signs of disturbance, then glared down at the Bar table and bared his fangs at me. 'You haven't called any other witnesses to corroborate your client's story,' he growled.

'Naturally, Y'r Honour,' I replied chirpily, 'I mean, if a woman is going to do away with her husband, she always makes sure there are no witnesses about. And if she is *not* going to do away with her husband,' I paused for effect, one eye on the judge, one eye on the jury: Then with a theatrical flourish of my right arm in the air, fist clenched, index finger outstretched, orated on, 'If she is not going to do away with her husband, there would be no reason at all for her to have any witnesses about...'

Again a pregnant pause for dramatic effect, ostentatiously patting the curls of my wig and gently smoothing the billowing folds of my gown. This carefully contrived moment of magic was unfortunately spoiled by a piercing wail from the dock, 'I didn't do away with him. I am innocent...'

'You did do away with him!' screeched her mother-in-law from the public gallery, 'You ain't innocent!'

Well, even Sir Laurence Olivier can't compete with a ladder dropped in the wings by some stage-hand. I glanced cautiously at the twelve solemn, severe faces there in the jury box, as bleak and merciless as the winds of Antarctica. Just my luck: My client is charged with murdering her husband, and I draw a jury composed entirely of *men*—all good, solid, self-righteous citizens, with hearts of pure granite.

With an elaborate shrug of resignation and a heavy histrionic sigh, I brushed a make-believe tear from my left eye and ploughed bravely on, 'Mr. Foreman and members of the Jury, the fate of the prisoner is in your hands. You twelve kindly, humane, compassionate, understanding, sympathetic citizens will no doubt laugh at the preposterous allegation that my unfortunate, downtrodden client poisoned her husband—'

'I want to be a witness,' again screeched the Accused's mother-in-law from the public gallery, 'My boy was the one who got lysol in his Lan Choo tea.'

'My wife uses Bushell's,' remarked the Crown Prosecutor.

'Really?' I sniffed superciliously, 'my wife uses nothing but Twinings.'

'Lan Choo is best,' called the Accused from the dock.

'Not with lysol in it,' screeched her mother-in-law from the public gallery.

'Silence in Court!' bellowed Mr Justice Broote.

The Foreman of the Jury, with cruel, cold eyes, thin lips, and that indefinable, implacable air of an habitual wife-beater, now leant forward and asked, 'What brand of disinfectant did she use to poison her husband?'

'She didn't poison her husband,' I protested indignantly.

'She did!' snorted the Crown Prosecutor.

'I didn't!' screamed the Accused.

'You did!' screeched her mother-in-law in the public gallery.

But His Honour had had enough. 'The Court will now adjourn,' he decided.

'All stand!' shouted his tipstaff.

Index finger outstretched

And with a flurry of scarlet and ermine and the swish of a full-bottomed wig, Mr Justice Broote disappeared from the bench like a Jack-in-the-box in reverse gear.

As I shuffled together the papers in my brief and fastened them securely with a strand of red tape, my instructing solicitor asked timidly, 'Will the jury find her Not Guilty?'

'What our client now needs,' I replied gloomily, 'is not so much the help of a barrister, as the help of the Almighty.' And with an access of religious fervour I hopefully rubbed the St. Jude medal pinned inside my Bar jacket.

I glanced at the solicitor, his brow furrowed with care—the poor chap had never learnt the secret of remaining detached from his clients' worries. No doubt he wouldn't get a wink of sleep all night. I smiled encouragingly at him, 'Things are sure to go better tomorrow.' But as a precaution I gave St. Jude, patron saint of lost causes, the Hope of the Hopeless, another brisk rub.

I returned to my Chambers, safe refuge from the slings and arrows of outrageous judges, and with a sigh of relief slipped off my gown, perched my wig neatly on the bald pate of a marble bust of Voltaire. After the tumult and the shouting of a day with Mr Justice Broote, it was a relief to be back again in my own familiar *pied à terre,* among the comfortable dark-red leather chairs, the polished gleam of the mahogany desk, walls lined with bookshelves from floor to ceiling, heavy red velvet drapes framing a large window which gazed directly across at the great dome towering above the Law Courts.

I stood at the window, glumly contemplating the Statue of Justice sitting silent, solitary and unsmiling above the entrance to the Supreme Court, and recalled Amy's dire warning at breakfast that morning: 'You must be careful today, Dominic,' she had said, as she placed before me a culinary disaster of lamb's fry and bacon, 'Your Stars are ill-omened. Aries is in opposition to Scorpio, and Taurus is entering the orbit of Aquarius.' My wife is a firm devotee of astrology. And not much of a cook, bless her.

Later, watching my desperate efforts to saw through a leathery strip of lamb's fry, she had repeated with all the prophetic melancholy of an Ides of March soothsayer accosting Caesar on his way to the Senate, 'You can't possibly win. Not today. Not with Taurus ascendant in Aquarius.'

What a way to start the morning—indigestion, and a jinx hanging around my neck!.

On my desk was a note from my clerk: Would I please phone my son Gerard? That only put me more out of sorts, so I just crumpled the note and tossed it into the waste-paper basket. Had I not done so, I might have avoided the shattering sequence of events which were about to overtake me.

To my eternal shame I must confess that I detest Gerard. Any paternal feelings of affection which I should by nature bear towards him have long since been extinguished. Probably since he was aged three and a half. He was a monster then and he is a monster now. A perpetual drain on my pocket.

The Christian Brothers shared my views. They expelled him.

Then, somehow or other Amy used influence to get him into Xavier. Well, the Jesuits have a reputation for being devious, but Gerard was more than a match for them. He became a champion footballer, so they just had to keep him on. By a miracle the Jesuits educated my son and heir to Matriculation, no doubt more due to the power of prayer on their part than to any effort on his.

'He is a Gemini,' Amy explained, 'Gemini people are difficult.'

Then the cost of putting him through medical school, with all the extra tuition that the Dean of the Faculty kept on assuring me was necessary in his case, and all those pressing and urgent summons from the Rector of Newman College, advising me that I was wasting my money and their time by keeping him on at the University, and why didn't I try to put him into some sort of a business instead, or send him to sea, or marry him off to some very rich girl . . . some very rich good Catholic girl, of course.

The astonishment of the Rector and of myself, when Gerard passed his final exams, was mutual.

'It is fortunate,' I remarked, 'that medical ethics preclude a doctor from attending members of his own family. The rest of the community may be at peril, but thank God, Amy and I are safe.'

The Rector nodded in distinct agreement.

Then there was the cost of setting the boy up in practice as a G.P. in South Yarra—a fashionable enough suburb for a budding medico, and he seemed to have some sort of charm for the rich elderly sick, but I made a point of never recommending him to any of our friends. I would rather they died of natural causes than from the medical maladministration of my incompetent offspring.

'Gerard has such a nice bedside manner,' old Mrs de Burgher said, but from what I heard, his bedside manner was even more admired by an endless succession of shrieking young long-legged females whom he drove around in that red MG with wire wheels, purchased by means of a loan (unrepaid) from me.

There was another note from my clerk on my desk. He had made an appointment for me to see a Mr Harry Pomfret, after court today.

'He wants to read law with you,' the note explained. 'He is well recommended.' Another budding barrister! I sighed. At that moment, half-way through a murder trial, with a grumpy old judge and a hard-hearted jury, I was scarcely in the mood for considering the credentials of some young turk fresh out of Law School, who wanted to become my apprentice.

I went looking for my clerk. He was out. He had gone to the funeral of one of the partners of a firm of solicitors who had died of heart failure after losing a case in which he had briefed me to appear. It had been all most unfortunate, very embarrassing. I had assured the solicitor that his client was a definite winner, that he need not worry about the recovery of the very large legal costs of the action, that it was a certainty.

Unfortunately we got the wrong judge, and the client turned out to be an out-and-out liar anyway, and as Amy remarked, 'What could you expect dear, with Virgo in conjuction with Libra?'

Anyway the solicitor died, and my clerk felt it incumbent on one of us to go to pay our final respects. We had decided better him than me, in the circumstances.

But who the devil was Harry Pomfret? And who had recommended him? Had I known the answer to those questions, had I known then what I know now, I would have without hesitation jumped from the window and probably landed on one of the solicitors' articled clerks scurrying along the street below. But I was at that time still an innocent, a lamb fit for the slaughter, completely ignorant of the identity of Harry Pomfret and of the Grand Guignol horrors he was about to dump on my doorstep.

Well—whoever he was—Harry Pomfret would have to wait, because I already had an urgent conference arranged, for a case later that week. That's the way it goes in the life of a barrister: always getting ready to fight the next case before you have even finished fighting the last one. A merry-go-round that never stops. A quarter-century of all that had taken some of the sparkle out of my step, had laced my hair with silver. Now, somewhat thicker in the waist, dependent on gold-rimmed spectacles to read the telephone book and the All England Law Reports, the sheer mental and emotional strain of fighting in Court all day and every day was slowly but surely starting to take its toll. Still, the show must go on—

My brief was to appear on behalf of one Emily Annie Artichoke, married woman. Her story was uninteresting:

Mrs Artichoke had wanted to spend a penny. Or rather, in these days of a revised and devalued currency: twenty cents. She had brought her husband into town on a shopping expedition, and they had become laden down with handy carry-bags, emblazoned brightly with the names of a varied assortment of merchandise and the suppliers thereof. The prospect of a long and jolting trip on the tram home had inspired Mrs Artichoke to seek sanctuary in the Ladies Rest-room of the Town Hall basement, leaving her husband standing at the tram stop, ankle-deep in a kaleidoscope of plastic bags.

In due course, feeling much relieved and able to face the world again without trepidation, Mrs Artichoke had attempted to leave the cubicle in which she was so snugly ensconced. To her surprise, and irritation, the door would not open. She shook it, banged at it with her handbag, took off her shoe and hit it, but the lock remained intractable.

'Yoo-hoo,' she called, 'Is anybody there?'

Silence.

'Yoo-hoo,' she called more loudly.

Silence.

Frustration gave way to dismay. 'Help!' she cried, her voice echoing loudly and hollowly around the tiled edifice in which she was entrapped.

'Help!' she cried again, and again, and again, but no welcome answering voice responded.

She was in a dilemma. She could wait, of course, until someone arrived, which hopefully would happen before sunset, but in the meantime her husband was left standing at the tram stop, with all those plastic shopping bags. So she decided to climb over the top of the door.

Now Mrs Artichoke was a sizeable woman, in fact quite fat, and hardly built for such enterprises as climbing over the top of lavatory doors. Still, nothing ventured, nothing won, so, firmly clutching her handbag, she placed one pudgy foot on the loo seat, another pudgy foot on the toilet-roll holder, and struggled to project herself out of her place of durance vile.

Unfortunately, at a crucial stage in her escape attempt the toilet-roll holder began to roll . . . and roll . . . and roll . . . sending Mrs Artichoke's right foot spinning, and spinning, and spinning, so that she fell heavily to the tiled floor, fractured her ankle, bruised her buttocks, and there she lay bedecked with innumerable metres of unrolled toilet paper.

Almost immediately two ladies entered the rest-room, heard her moans of despair and pushed the door open, crushing three of her fingers in their rescue operation.

Which is how Mrs Artichoke and her spouse, with their solicitor, now came to be sitting in my Chambers, lamenting her sad experience, and urging me to take the Lord Mayor, Councillors and Citizens of the City of Melbourne to the cleaners for every penny they had.

'It ain't right,' she complained bitterly, 'leaving me shut up there, and my husband standing waiting at the tram stop, wondering what. It ain't right.'

I stifled a yawn. After a hard day in court, with Mr Justice Broote mumbling and grumbling like Mt Etna about to erupt, and with a hand-picked bunch of male chauvinist misogynists for a jury—I stifled another yawn.

'Can you win my case?' Mrs Artichoke demanded, sizing me up with a baleful stare.

'Yes,' I replied and their faces became wreathed in smiles.

'And no,' I continued, and the smiles gave way to perplexity and then to downright hostility.

'What do you mean—yes and no?' protested her husband, who

had obviously in his imagination already spent the proceeds of his wife's forthcoming litigation.

'Well, the defendants must pay damages,' I remarked, and again they smiled. 'Less—'

'Less what?'

'Less contributory negligence—own fault trying to climb over door—reckless behavior—endangering own safety—' and the smiles once more became scowls.

'I will see you again on the morning of the trial,' I nodded soothingly to their solicitor, 'Good afternoon.' And they wafted out, mumbling to one another.

Which still left that young would-be barrister to be interviewed before I could go home to more of Amy's burnt offerings, bless her. *Kissing don't last; cooking do!* wrote the novelist George Meredith. He too must have married an Amy . . .

'Your name?' I asked the young man, by way of openers.

'Harry Pomfret sir,' he replied gravely. Fair, crinkly hair (too long of course, but clean and well brushed), pale grey eyes, trim athletic build, he wore a three-piece suit which was certainly not new, though carefully pressed. The shirt collar and cuffs were heavily starched, just starting to fray. Shrewdly sizing him up, I guessed that all he had going for him were youth and ambition, without any family backing to subsidize him through those early lean and impoverished years which are the inevitable lot of an aspiring barrister.

'I understand you want to read law with me.'

'Yes, please.'

'Well, I'd better find out something about you, I suppose, before we come to any firm decision on that.' (Whoever had recommended him? Perhaps one of my staunch solicitor supporters. I must be careful not to offend.)

'Where did you study law?' I enquired.

'Monash University.' (That was a bad start. The students agitate at Monash, I believe.)

'Honours degree?'

'I'm afraid not. Just a pass.'

'A pass degree is not a very adequate qualification for a career at the Bar,' I remarked, now really perplexed as to the identity of his recommender. 'What school?'

'Coburg High.'

I blinked again now. A State School! And on the wrong side of the Yarra too. That meant he would be without any connections, probably had never played cricket.

'Do you go to Church?' I asked, with assumed disinterest.

'Catholic,' he flashed me a knowing smile. I was not then aware (how could I be?) that the versatile Harry Pomfret changed his religion as easily and as regularly as he changed his socks, all according to the company he was in.

'Any political affiliations?'

'True blue Liberal.' (His politics I later learnt were as chameleon as his religion, but for the moment his answer somewhat reassured me.)

'Do you know any solicitors, anyone who might send you briefs if you come to the Bar?'

He looked at me earnestly. 'I am working on it,' he replied, and left me in no doubt that he was indeed.

'What does your father do?' I asked.

He went to speak, stopped, then, 'I haven't got a father. Not to speak of, anyway.'

'Why not? Is he in gaol?'

Harry looked at me thoughtfully, and answered, 'My father is a judge—' He stopped short, in an embarrassed manner.

I frowned. 'There is no Mr Justice Pomfret that I know of.'

Again the embarrassed hesitation. 'I was born on the wrong side of the blanket, as the saying is,' he volunteered.

Now it was my turn to be embarrassed.

'Humph . . . Mm . . . Yes, yes,' I replied. So that explained my clerk's note that young Pomfret came well recommended. I wondered which of the Supreme Court judiciary had been the naughty boy. Well, whoever it was, seeing he had sent his by-blow for me to complete his education, I had better oblige. To refuse might have been unpleasant repercussions next time I appeared in a case before that judge. Perhaps unpleasant repercussions *in perpetuum*.

'I think I can take you as a pupil,' I conceded, and the young man's face lighted up with relief and pleasure. 'But first you will have to make arrangements with my clerk, and obtain the approval of the Bar Council.'

'When would you suggest I start?'

'Let's say, in a fortnight. That should give you ample time

to settle everything. You will have to acquire a wig, and robes. My clerk will explain all that to you.'

As he was leaving, I enquired, 'How old are you?'

'Twenty-four.'

'I have a son of your age,' I remarked, by way of conversation.

'Yes, I know,' he smiled, and closed the door before I had any opportunity to pursue the subject. But the rejoinder left me somewhat uneasy. Anyone who knows Gerard, anyone on even a nodding acquaintance with Gerard, must be suspect in my opinion . . .

After a long hard day in court with Mr Justice Broote and the twelve merciless men, I thought I might manage a quick Scotch before I left for *Chez Amy* and her inevitable platter of batter, bless her. As I turned into the Four Courts Hotel, I noticed my clerk sitting in a corner, alone.

'Nice wake, Arthur?' I asked, as I joined him.

'There was no wake,' he replied gloomily. 'They all just went home.'

'Pity.'

'Did you phone Master Gerard?' he enquired.

'No, I was too busy. I had a conference for that trial later this week.'

'Did Harry Pomfret turn up?'

'Yes . . . Tell me, Arthur, who recommended him?'

'Why, young Master Gerard. He knew him at the University.'

I bit my lip. Hook, line and sinker! But—'But that's not possible. Gerard was at Melbourne University and young Pomfret went to Monash.'

'Well, Master Gerard just said that he knew him when he was at the University. I suppose that could be. Did you agree to take him as a pupil?'

I nodded grimly and finished off my Scotch. Arthur had always had a soft spot for Gerard, but really, the idea of taking a Reader who was a friend of my son filled me with the direst foreboding.

Which foreboding proved to be only too correct. But the die was cast. The sword of Damocles was already poised above my head.

WHICH JUDGE IS MY FATHER?

My enquiries disclosed that Gerard had indeed known young Pomfret when he was at the University. They had bumped into one another—literally—during an Inter-Varsity football match, an event which had seen them both carted off by ambulance to St Vincent's Hospital, both with knee injuries, and both admitted for immediate surgery at the hands of the Orthopaedic Department.

Each now minus a cartilage, they had been placed in the same ward, in adjoining beds, and had struck up a friendship.

I hadn't bothered to visit Gerard at St Vincent's—indeed I have been kept busy working twice as hard at my legal practice in order to pay the astronomical accounts which the good Sisters of Charity kept sending me: Item—in-patient fees; Item—Anaesthetist's fees; Item—analgesics; Item—crepe bandages; Item—hire of crutches; etc. etc., all to the greater glory of God and to the descending debit of my bank balance.

However, Amy had visited Gerard, and I recalled her babbling on about 'such a nice boy in the next bed. He is a Pisces . . .', quite unmoved by my peevish grumbling that the clumsiness of that nice boy in the next bed was now costing me a small fortune.

'It's your own fault, Dominic,' she retorted. 'If you hadn't forgotten to pay the Medical Benefits subscription, it wouldn't have cost you anything.'

She was right, of course. Amy always is right, bless her. It's very difficult being married to a woman who is always right. Amy is not only always right, but she always tells me she is always right. Which is all wrong, in my opinion. It is very wearing.

After their discharge from hospital, Gerard and Harry Pomfret had kept in touch, had gone together to watch the football and the drag-racing out at the speedway, had got drunk together at the University Hotel, had lost money together at the two-up school at North Fitzroy, together had chased an obliging pack of women students from the Arts Faculty and, in short, had encouraged one another in all those extra-curricular activities which preoccupy the leisure hours of undergraduate Sawbones and Legal Eagles.

In my University days, distance and the necessity of going everywhere by public transport would have soon killed such a friendship stone-dead, but in these modern times the campuses of Melbourne and Monash are only a cup of petrol away. Gerard had a beat-up old second-hand VW I had bought him. Young Pomfret whizzed around on a put-put bike, though it apparently splut-spluttered more often than it put-putted. They had the same interests: sport, alcohol, the lure of the women students of Janet Clarke Hall, leaving them just enough time for an occasional, teeny-weeny peek at their University text-books—barely sufficient for them to scrape through with pass degrees in their respective Faculties.

Gerard had never mentioned Harry Pomfret to me, but that was hardly surprising. Whenever I saw Gerard, I was obliged to spend all my time pontificating about how he must study harder, or else I would be forced to take him away from University. That sort of conversation hardly engenders confidential exchanges about the wild friends of one's youth.

The morning young Pomfret arrived at my Chambers to commence his apprenticeship, I immediately sent him off to get his hair cut.

'If you hope to be a successful barrister,' I remarked, 'you might as well look like one, and not be mistaken for some impecunious criminal ruffian client of mine on Legal Aid.'

He went off to be shorn, without protest, which was a promising start, anyway. Gerard was never so compliant to such requests. Little did I then suspect that this obedient lamb would turn out to be a wolf in sheep's clothing.

When Pomfret returned, Arthur settled him down at a desk, gave him some dusty volumes of law reports to look at.

'They've got no pictures in them,' I observed. 'Can you read?'

He smiled nervously. The first day in Chambers is like the

first day at school. Of course nobody pours an inkwell over the new boy's head or puts a tack on his seat, but the welcome accorded him is reserved and lukewarm. Every barrister to whom he is introduced mouths cordial Good-lucks, but all that polite veneer is tempered by caution. For this Johnny-come-lately is a potential threat to every other member of the Bar: one day, sooner or later, he must be faced in Court, and fought. In the meantime, every man takes his measure, patronizes him, subtly assures him of his inferiority, of his abysmal ignorance in matters of law, of the certainty that he will be a hopeless failure.

'I have to go over to the Criminal Court to make a plea,' I said, as I put on my gown, shrugged it into shape, and adjusted my wig. 'You might as well come with me, and see how it is done.'

Pomfret again smiled nervously, and followed at a respectful distance. I don't think he learnt much though, because I had the misfortune to appear before one of our more elderly judges, well past his prime, and with the unnerving habit of nodding off half way through proceedings.

'According to your Stars in the morning paper,' Amy had warned me, 'today you must beware of misunderstandings.'

My client on this occasion was a useless young brute who had knocked down a 70-year-old pensioner and stolen her purse, containing one dollar and forty-seven cents.

'Prisoner at the bar,' the Judge's Associate announced in loud ringing tones, 'you have pleaded guilty to a charge of robbery with violence. Have you anything to say why sentence should not be passed upon you?'

So I got up and began a fiercely impassioned plea about how my most unfortunate client was the sole support of his poor old most unfortunate mother, and how his father had deserted them when my poor unfortunate client was still sucking at his mother's poor unfortunate breast—all the usual heart-rending sob-stuff. As I perorated on and on, the learned Judge blinked, and yawned, and blinked, and yawned, and in due course nodded off as usual.

When I finally finished speaking, His Honour, awoken with a start by the sudden silence and not quite knowing what was going on, ordered the immediate release of my client and sentenced the 70-year-old pensioner to 28 days in gaol. By the time we had got that all sorted out, the poor soul was off in the paddy-wagon, half-way to the Women's Prison at Fairlea. It no doubt gave her quite a shock.

I had, during the preceding fortnight, given some thought to the possible identity of Pomfret's progenitor. I had discarded the Chief Justice as a suspect. A fat podgy little man with a bald head—and he had been since as far back as I could remember, almost from the time he left school. And a Methodist. He probably didn't even know how to spell the word *adultery*. But that still left a sizeable line-up of perhaps putative parents.

I decided that the best thing to do, to assuage my curiosity, was to confront Pomfret directly, and to have the matter out.

'You mentioned that your father is a judge,' I remarked, off-hand.

He looked steadfastly at me, but said nothing.

I cleared my throat. 'Which judge is your father?' I asked.

'I don't know.'

'What do you mean, you don't know?'

And he told me his story:

He and his mother had lived alone, in a small Housing Commission flat. She had a cleaning job, four days a week, but her meagre earnings were supplemented by the regular arrival of a cheque in a plain envelope. Harry was never allowed to see these cheques, so he had no idea from whom they came, or for how much, but his curiosity was aroused when on one occasion the bottom left-hand corner of the envelope bore the legend:

Judges' Chambers
Supreme Court
Melbourne

His mother had turned a deaf ear to his questions, and there the matter had rested.

All he knew of his origins was, from a chance remark by his mother, that he had been conceived at the Pig and Whistle Hotel, somewhere in the Blue Mountains in New South Wales. He also knew that he had been a full-term baby, so by some simple arithmetic, he was able to deduce that his conception had been during the Queen's Birthday weekend holiday in 1956. For young Pomfret this was the only clue which might one day lead to the discovery of the identity of his hitherto unknown male parent.

His mother had displayed unusual ambition in matters of

Harry's future, always urging him on, and his school exam results reflected her determination. But from the word go, she had consistently assured Harry that when he grew up he must be a lawyer, must be a barrister, perhaps one day be a judge, like someone or other she had once known. In due course she saw the beginnings of the realization of her dreams, when Harry was enrolled at Law School and ultimately graduated.

But before she could see the complete fulfilment of her ambitions, Harry's mother fell ill with what appeared to be a minor ailment. Harry had, of course, called in his friendly neighbourhood quack, his good friend Gerard.

A mistake, I thought to myself, a terrible mistake. It was a wonder she survived.

Despite Gerard's assiduous attention and medical care, Harry went on, his mother had died.

I knew it! I knew it! I should have enrolled him in Veterinary Science, not Medicine. If only I had made him an animal doctor instead of turning him loose on the human race!

When he realized that his mother was about to go to her eternal reward, Harry saw the only chance of discovering the secret of his ancestry slipping through his fingers. At the last moment, summoning up his courage, he had leant over his mother and whispered, 'But who is my father?'

The dying women had looked at him uncertainly, and not replied.

Again he whispered, 'Mother, who is my father?'

Her lips moved but no sound came.

Desperately he repeated the question once again, and, rallying her last vestiges of remaining strength, she gasped hoarsely, 'Your father is . . . '

'Yes?' he encouraged her.

'Your father is . . . is . . . a judge . . . '

'But which judge?' he asked. 'Which judge is my father?'

The only response was a death rattle, and he appeared forever deprived of the last link to the enigma of his origins.

'And now I shall probably never know,' he concluded lamely.

I sat contemplating him for a few minutes, pondering. Then I made my first fatal mistake—busying myself in the problem of Pomfret's parentage! I little suspected where that search would lead, that the administration of justice in the State of Victoria was about to be convulsed to its very foundations.

'How long ago was it that the Supreme Court envelope arrived?' I innocently asked at last.

'Eight years, perhaps nine. At least eight anyway.'

'Well, that chops out any judges appointed in the last eight years, doesn't it? It narrows the field a little.'

'I suppose so, but—'

'Look, if you really want to find out, it is no use sitting around like Patience on a monument. Make a few enquiries.'

'Such as?'

I went to my bookshelves and took down a copy of *Who's Who*. Opening the pages, I looked up at random the name of one of the remaining judges. I glanced at the entry, and handed it to the young man.

'There's another one out of the running. By a coincidence, he was married that weekend, Queen's Birthday 1956. I don't think he would have been rushing off to the Blue Mountains to beget you.'

Harry's eyes narrowed, thoughtfully. 'What would you suggest I do?'

'Go to the Public Library and look up all the old newspapers of the period—the *SUN,* the *AGE* and the *ARGUS.*' I considered. 'Oh, and the *HERALD,* and *TRUTH.* Read through every edition for the week before and the week after the Queen's Birthday.'

'What shall I look for?'

'See if any big trials were reported, extending over that fortnight. If they were, make a note of the names of all the barristers appearing in the cases, and we will check whether any of them have since been elevated to the Bench.'

'But what will that prove?'

'If there was a long trial, the barristers would have been busy in Melbourne all weekend, working on the case. A barrister's social life plays second fiddle to his professional career. When you are in the middle of a trial, you don't just disappear off to some Pig and Whistle pub for the weekend. You are hard at it, here in Chambers, or in your study at home, Saturday and Sunday, getting ready to resume battle next week.'

Young Pomfret did as I suggested, and his researches bore

fruit. There had in fact been a *cause célèbre* litigated that month, a libel action, arising out of an article in the *ARGUS* headed ARCHBISHOP'S LURID LITTLE LOVE-NEST, and a bevy of Silks and a battalion of Junior Counsel had been briefed to slog it out. By comparing the names, we were able to eliminate four more judges from the list of suspects.

Pomfret even found one more bonus news item: another of the present judges, who in those days had political aspirations, had that very weekend addressed a branch meeting of the members of the Liberal Party at Prahran. So that was another one we could forget about.

I had made some enquiries myself and was able to inform my pupil that a further two of the judges, then eminent Q.C.'s, had been in London for several months in mid-1956, arguing an Appeal before the Privy Council.

When we had collated all this information, and narrowed it down to possibilities, six names only remained on the list:

Mr Justice Applebaum
Sir Frederick Kneebone
Mr Justice Melchior
Mr Justice Philanderer
Sir Anthony Opscotch
Mr Justice Cumquat

And a fine bunch of scallywags they were—or had been in their hey-day. Any one of them could have been the culprit.

'The most likely among that motley crew,' I said, casting my eye down the names, 'would be Mr Justice Melchior.'

'But he's so very old,' protested Pomfret.

'He wasn't very old twenty-five years ago,' I retorted. 'Not too old to sneak off for a dirty weekend with some popsy. He had a reputation. Perhaps by now he is an extinct volcano, but there may even still be a few rumbles left in the old crater. Yes, Melchior is probably your sire.'

So Harry Pomfret, budding barrister-at-law, began to prepare a dossier on the love-life of the Honourable Mr Justice Melchior.

Several days later, I took my pupil to help me look up some cases in the Law Times Reports in the Supreme Court Library. In a cobbled courtyard in the centre of the Law Courts stands a round tower, built of rich sandstone, reaching high, high up into the heavens and surmounted and encircled by a forest of classical stone columns, supporting a great dome. This round tower houses the Library where you may always find a sprinkling of barristers, poring over volumes of law reports that date back to 1220. The floor is thickly carpeted, on the walls hang oil paintings of gone and long-forgotten Chief Justices, and there is an air of scholarly calm throughout. The busy traffic of William Street is only a stone's throw away, but no sound penetrates these thick strong walls, no member of the public sees inside.

There, for several hours, Pomfret and I worked silently, poring over precedents, tracing a tricky legal argument from one volume of Law Reports to another: A seventeen-year-old country lad had beaten up his poor old mother, putting her into hospital in a coma for several months. He evaded apprehension by the police and fled to Melbourne, where he squatted in an empty derelict house. Then, one rainy night a mongrel dog took refuge on the front door-mat of this house. Early the next morning, awoken by the rattle of milk bottles, the dog ran out of the front gate of the house and bit a milkman on the behind, so savagely that the victim required reconstructive plastic surgery. The milkman of course wanted to sue somebody, but whom?

With Pomfret, I searched through the Law Reports, making copious notes, comparing the decision of one judge in 1670 with the decision of another judge in 1792, then with the decision of a third judge in 1845, gradually building up a dossier from which I hoped to be able to predict with some certainty what a judge would decide in this Year of Grace. At last I was satisfied.

'We'll sue the comatose old mother!' I announced triumphantly, 'and sell up her house to recover the milkman's damages, probably before the old lady has even recovered consciousness.'

Young Pomfret gazed at me in bewilderment as I rubbed my hands in glee. 'The law, like God, moves in a mysterious way its wonders to perform,' I reassured him, 'and the Dog Act is a fine example of those wondrous mysteries.'

As Pomfret still continued to look dumbly at me, totally nonplussed, I explained my process of reasoning in very simple terms, so that he would be sure to understand: 'The seventeen-year- old was occupying the derelict house, and the dog ran out of those premises. Right?' He nodded, and I continued, '*Ergo* and *ipso facto* and *a priori* the youth is presumed to be the owner of the dog — *stabit praesumptio donec probetur in contrarium.* But a seventeen-year-old is a minor at law and *doli incapax durante minore aetate.* So the Dog Act conveniently decrees that his parent *qui per alium facit per seipsum facere videtur* will be deemed *ex delicto* responsible *per actionem noxalem* for the milkman's bitten behind. *Quod erat demonstrandum : Cani boro iorum brella?'* I smiled encouragingly at my pupil. 'No doubt the old mother will be somewhat surprised when she comes out of Intensive Care. She may even have a relapse.'

As we were making our way back to Chambers, whom should we meet but Mr Justice Melchior, returning from lunch at the Australian Club.

'Good afternoon, Dominic,' he said in his now rather frail but still well modulated voice, 'Nice day, ain't it? Is that your new Reader? I heard you'd taken someone on.'

I introduced them.

'Good luck, young fellow, good luck. I don't think I've ever seen you around before. What's your background, eh?'

Harry looked him challengingly in the eye, 'I was conceived at the Pig and Whistle on the Queen's Birthday, 1956.'

There was a silence. Melchior's eyes widened, his jaw gaped slightly, and he glanced at me, his eyebrows slightly raised.

'H'm,' he said at last, and turned and tottered off to the private entrance of Judges' Chambers.

'What do you think?' Pomfret asked. 'He seemed taken off balance, didn't he?'

I nodded agreement, but added, 'I'm not sure that such a bald statement of fact would not startle whomsoever.'

In short, I considered Melchior's reaction quite equivocal.

PHONE A DOCTOR!

The following Sunday morning Amy and I decided that, for a change, we would go to Mass at Our Lady of Victories. The 8 a.m. at O.L.V. is always very legal, with a smattering of judges, quite a few Counsel and many solicitors.

To my surprise and delight, I noticed Harry Pomfret down in the second row from the front, very conspicuous. After Mass I looked for him, to introduce him to Amy, but couldn't find him anywhere.

That afternoon a friend and I went for a round of golf at the Royal Melbourne, and as we were hitting off at the seventh tee, we were overtaken by Mr Justice Kneebone whose main claim to fame is that he plays to a handicap of 4.

'Nice day, Dominic,' he greeted me. 'Saw that new pupil of yours at Church this morning.'

'Where?' I enquired, puzzled.

'St John's of course. Ten o'clock Matins. Seems a fine young man.'

Now St John's, as you no doubt know, is the praying place of the Church of England judges and is always liberally patronised by well-to-do Anglican solicitors.

My bewilderment was even further compounded as I strolled towards Chambers the next morning.

'Your Reader has a very good singing voice,' Macquarie Q.C. remarked. 'He was at the 9 o'clock service at St Stephen's. A good lad.'

So my pupil had also embraced Presbyterianism!

When I entered my Chambers, Pomfret was sitting there, hard at work on some Interrogatories which I had asked him to draft. I am afraid my good morning greeting was far from cordial.

I settled down to read my brief for the day. An uncomfortable silence prevailed.

At last I could contain myself no longer. I left my desk and went to him. 'I noticed you at 8 o'clock Mass yesterday,' I said.

He looked up and smiled sweetly. 'Yes,' he replied.

'Macquarie Q.C. also noticed you at the 9 o'clock service at the Presbyterian Church,' I went on.

Pomfret's eyes were suddenly glued to his work. 'Yes,' he replied.

'Mr Justice Kneebone also noticed you at 10 o'clock Matins at the Church of England,' I continued.

'Mm.'

There was a long pause.

'How can you do it?' I enquired at last, reproachfully.

'I have a motor bike,' he explained, still intent on his work.

'And I suppose you also play the drum in the Salvation Army?' I retorted with more than an edge of sarcasm in my voice.

Now Pomfret looked up with great interest. 'I didn't know any solicitors belonged to the Salvation Army?' he asked eagerly.

Words failed me and I retreated to my desk.

They say that you can't put an old head on young shoulders, but by the end of that day Harry Pomfret had received briefs from three Catholic solicitors, four Anglicans and two Presbyterians.

The briefs were, for the most part, only to defend clients on minor traffic charges—exceeding the speed limit, driving through the red lights, the sort of thing solicitors let a new barrister cut his teeth on until they have reassured themselves that he can be safely entrusted with more weighty matters. Still, small fish are sweet, and nine briefs in the one day for a young man newly called to the Bar was an achievement not to be sniffed at.

One of the briefs however caught my eye. The Accused was a hardened criminal with a list of prior convictions as long as your arm. This time he was to be presented for trial on charges of factory breaking and being armed with an offensive weapon. That, certainly, was not the job for a novice barrister.

I browsed through the papers. The jury trial was to be presided over by none other than His Honour Mr Justice Melchior. Now that could be interesting, if judge and Counsel for the Defence were a father and son team!

His main claim to fame

As I glanced hurriedly at the depositions taken at the Committal Proceedings, I became instinctively uneasy. After a few years at this game, you can smell a rat a mile off. The only substantial evidence against the Accused lay in the deposition of three small-time crooks, all of whom swore that the Accused had told them he was the one who had broken into the factory. He had shown them (so they said) the pistol he had taken with him at the time. Significantly, absolutely none of the stolen property had been recovered.

The case had all the classic earmarks of a frame-up, and the Accused would need more experienced Counsel than young Pomfret if the evidence that had been cooked up against him was to be exposed.

I was about to tell Pomfret to advise the solicitors who had sent him the brief that he was not yet ready for that sort of case, when I had second thoughts about the matter. In view of the shocking duplicity of his behaviour, motor-cycling from church to church just to impress solicitors in the hope of picking up a few briefs, it would be only fit and proper to leave him to flounder in a trial well beyond his skill and experience.

Of course, as his Master, I would have to help him prepare the case, advise him how to run it, warn him of the pitfalls, but when it came to the crunch he would be on his own, to sink or swim. I had no doubt at all that he would sink, but that would be a well-merited lesson for him. Yes, I would let him keep the brief—

'Before Mr Justice Melchior!' he exclaimed excitedly. 'Perhaps I could work some sort of question into the cross-examination which would be a hidden signal to the judge that I now know his secret, that he is my father.'

'You may try,' I commented wryly, 'but I imagine you will have enough on your plate defending the Accused, without furthering your own schemes.'

Of course I had not taken his remark seriously. I little realized that before long his stubbon determination to flush out his father was to send Her Majesty's very honourable and very upright Justices ducking for cover in all directions.

Over the next four days I put Pomfret through a crash course in Court etiquette: when to bow to the presiding judge; the correct angle of inclination—not too low, not too casual; to remember to murmur politely, 'If Y'r Honour pleases' before commencing cross-examination; to stand when spoken to by the judge; not to smile ingratiatingly at the jury; to speak up loudly so that everybody could hear him . . . all the little bread-and-butter touches that are part of an advocate's daily life.

'But the main thing,' I counselled, 'is that you are not entitled to have a private opinion of your own as to your client's guilt or innocence. He has pleaded Not Guilty and that is the end of the matter. He is accordingly entitled to be defended to your utmost ability, no matter how overwhelming the evidence against him may appear to be.'

On the day before the trial was to commence, Pomfret and I went over once again the depositions in the case.

'Who are the most dangerous witnesses against your client?' I catechised him.

'The three who say that the Accused told them he broke into the factory.'

'Why are they dangerous?'

'Because their evidence has been concocted.'

'What consequence flows from that?'

'I must assume that they have been carefully drilled in how to give their evidence in Court.'

'Good,' I commended him. 'Now hear this: Not only will those witnesses have their story off pat, but they will also have been alerted to the type of question you will ask them in cross-examination.'

'Then I must endeavour to take them by surprise.' He was an apt pupil.

'And how will you do that?'

'The first question I ask must be calculated to upset them, to make them uneasy and throw them out of their stride, so that the story they have made up will start to become unstuck.'

'If you do that, young Pomfret,' I nodded, 'I will be proud of you.'

At the first Oscar Wilde trail, when he sued the Marquess of Queensberry for defamation, Wilde's evidence-in-chief went swimmingly and completely won the hearts of the jury. But when the famous Carson Q.C. arose to cross-examine, his immediate question was: 'You stated that your age was thirty-nine. I think you are over forty?' and Carson held aloft a copy of Wilde's birth certificate.

It was a devastating opening. Wilde had told a silly unimportant lie, but in one fell swoop his credit was shattered, his self-possession began to crumble, and the jury became suspicious. It was Wilde's first step on the path to Reading Gaol.

Over dinner that night, as I chewed and chewed on a piece of rock-hard baked potato, I mentioned to Amy that my Reader had his first trial tomorrow. She immediately consulted the evening paper.

'He is a Pisces,' she muttered, running her finger down the column of astrological portents and predictions and then reading: 'Tomorrow will be for you a day of happy reunions.'

Happy reunions? Perhaps, I thought, it was no mere coincidence but the hand of fate that had led Mr Justice Melchior to preside over Pomfret's first trial. I was reminded of those Perry Mason shows on T.V. where, at a crucial point in the proceedings, someone suddenly stood up at the back of the Court and shouted, 'I did it! I did it! The defendant is innocent. I am the murderer!' . . . Could it be that in the middle of Pomfret's first case the learned trial judge would suddenly jump from his chair, leap over the Bench, bound down to the Bar table and embrace Counsel for the Defence, confessing with tears in his eyes, 'My son, my own son! I am your long-lost father!'

No that would be too long a shot. Besides, Melchior was a bit old for too much leaping and bounding.

When I arrived in Chambers the next morning, my pupil was busy in front of the small looking-glass which hung near the entrance door, battling to force his shirt studs through the stud-holes of a heavily-starched wing collar. Once you are experienced in this routine daily task it takes a moment only, but for the nervously trembling fingers of a newly-fledged Counsel it requires gargantuan effort. And the addition of each new article of apparel makes him more and more nervous. The wig is always the final devastating blow to his self-confidence.

Of course, a baby barrister invariably adopts an air of bravado as if the wearing of robes is nothing extraordinary, but beneath all that superficial *savoir faire* his heart is pounding flitter-flutter in a paroxysm of pleasure and embarrassment. Only time and experience can reconcile him to the oddity of his appearance.

For myself, when I change into my Bar jacket each morning, put on my wing collar and bands, then finally my gown, it is no different from a tradesman putting on his overalls. These are my working clothes and I feel comfortable in them, like in an old coat or a pair of gardening pants. I never think about them, never wonder what I look like, I just know that I am ready for work, properly garbed, and into battle! Indeed, I would feel most awkward fighting a case in a three-piece suit.

But with my wig, it is a different matter. We have been together a long time, that wig and I. When I was a young and uncouth barrister, making more mistakes than you would believe possible, my wig was a sparkling pristine white. It was made for me in England, by Ede and Ravenscroft, who have outfitted barristers and judges with their crowning glory from time immemorial, plucking tufts of pure white hair from the manes and tails of pure white horses.

In the 18th Century, when most men wore wigs, the lawyers did not. Then, when the habit of wearing wigs was dying out, the lawyers, with their usual contrariness, began to do so. We have always had a reputation for being behind the times. But we improved on the wigs. Instead of using human hair, forever requiring combing and setting, we had them made of horse-hair, and set in a severe and rigid permanent style, needing little care and attention.

In my first days at the Bar, I was continually and distractingly conscious of a wig on my head. It was uncomfortable, the horse-hair made my scalp itchy, it made my head hot in the warm weather . . . But gradually we have become accustomed to one another, that wig and I, until now it is more part of me than my own hair. Slowly the whiter-than-white horse-hair, by some mysterious alchemy of ageing, has turned grey, as also have I, and you would be hard put to determine where the wig stops and my own hair starts.

Each morning, last thing before I leave for Court, I glance in the mirror to make sure my wig is sitting straight on my head and it gives me a comforting feeling to see it there, firm, precise, ready for the day's fray. We have been through a lot together, through drama, excitement and tragedy, when the air in Court has been so charged with emotion that one almost chokes.

Together we have suffered humiliating defeats and judicial snubs, experienced glorious triumphs and the joys of victory.

When I at last one day hang up my gown and Bar jacket, and Amy and I retire to some small holiday house by the seaside, that wig will come with me, snug in its little travelling case emblazoned with scrolls and whirls, to remind me of the good times and the bad times, the gay days and the grey days. This little patch of horse-hair, so meticulously sewn together by some now forgotten craftsman, is a symbol of my life at the Bar. It is my most precious possession.

I was hard at work writing an Opinion on Easements and Estovers, when Pomfret came into my room. Engrossed in my thoughts, I was unaware of his entry and glanced up in surprise when he asked, 'How do I look?'

He looked well.On this first occasion that he had worn a wig and gown, I knew the thoughts that must have been running through his head—a little vanity, a lot of nervousness, the uncontrollable terror that everybody would be staring at him. Wearing robes for the first time really is not easy.

'How do I look?' he repeated, smiling uneasily.

I stood up and went around to the front of my desk, slowly circled him once, smoothing out a drape here, a fold there. It was so like the old days, inspecting Gerard when he first went to school.

'Show me the back of your hands and your fingernails,' I demanded.

He had obviously been through all that in his early days too, because automatically the hands went out for my inspection. Then he realized it was a joke, and laughed shyly.

Suddenly I felt ashamed of myself. I should not have let him keep that brief, should not have allowed this boy to go on a man's errand. At the moment he was all eagerness and anticipation. By the end of the trial he would probably wish he were dead. And what if Melchior savaged him, on his very first trial? It would not be the first time Melchior had broken a young barrister's confidence.

However, the die was cast now. I had let Pomfret get himself into this predicament, and could only hope for the best.

'Good luck, boy,' I said, and patted him reassuringly on the shoulder. As he reached the door, I stopped him. 'Don't panic.

Whatever you do, don't panic.' And I added, 'I shall stroll over to Court and watch you perform, if I have time.'

When he was gone, I went slowly back to my desk and muttered half a dozen Hail Marys.

When I finally made my way over to the court where he was appearing, it was with great apprehension. Still, if Pomfret was going to be mangled, I had better be there to pick up the pieces.

The Crown Prosecutor had just finished his opening address, and the first witness was called. This was one of the conspirators, and almost immediately it became apparent that he really had been very well schooled in what he was to say. His answers were so pertinent and precise, so carefully phrased and pronounced, that their effect on the jury would be certain.

I glanced at the jury. They were leaning forward, rapt, taking in every word.

I looked at old Melchior. He too appeared impressed, pursing his lips in that soundless whistle shape which he adopted on those rare occasions when he whole-heartedly believed the evidence of a witness.

'This trial would have been difficult enough for me,' I thought, 'but it is an impossibility for an inexperienced novice.'

When the witness had completed his evidence-in-chief and the Crown Prosecutor had resumed his seat with a satisfied and complacent air, Pomfret stood up.

'If Y'r Honour pleases,' he murmured. Well, at least he got that part right . . .

Melchior smiled encouragingly and Pomfret turned to the witness.

His first question certainly did take the witness by surprise. It also took the Crown Prosecutor by surprise, and the Judge, and the jury, also His Honour's Associate, and the tipstaff, even the policeman on duty at the door of the Court.

'Were you,' Pomfret began in a loud clear voice, holding one finger up in the air and glancing sideways at the Judge, 'Were you at the Pig and Whistle Hotel on the Queen's Birthday weekend in 1956?'

I groaned inwardly.

The witness, who thought he knew beforehand every question he was likely to be asked by Defence Counsel, was nonplussed and stammered for an answer.

Melchior leaned forward, obviously under the impression that he had misunderstood what had been asked. 'What exactly was that question, Mr Pomfret?'

Now turning directly towards the Judge, and again holding one finger upright, Pomfret repeated, 'Were you at the Pig and Whistle Hotel on the Queen's Birthday weekend in 1956?'

Melchior's reaction was interesting. For one minute he sat there in amazement. Then his nose began to twitch in bewilderment and he sank back into his chair with a puzzled frown. After a few seconds' further consideration, during which time he was obviously engrossed in deep thought, he suddenly came to.

'Well,' he thundered at the witness, 'answer the question. Were you?'

'No, your Honour. I wasn't.'

'H'mm!' growled Melchior, and that H'm made it quite clear to the jury that he and they had obviously been much mistaken about the confidence they should place in this witness. 'H'mm.'

That first surprise question certainly worked like a charm. After it, the witness was putty in Pomfret's hands. He stuttered and spluttered, forgot his lines, contradicted himself, said he had a headache and could he go home?

The second witness fared no better.

'Were you,' Pomfret asked uncompromisingly, one finger erect, 'at the Pig and Whistle Hotel on the Queen's Birthday weekend in 1956?'

When this witness also admitted that he was not, Melchior exchanged a knowing glance with the jury, and the jury exchanged knowing glances with one another, and the policemen at the door nodded wisely as if he had suspected that all along.

As the third conspirator entered the witness box to give evidence, the Foreman of the Jury was heard to remark in a loud voice, 'I'll bet he wasn't there either.'—which perspicacious remark earned him a confirmatory nod of approval from the Judge.

'No,' answered the witness, and added, 'I ain't never been there.'

This additional information caused quite a buzz of comment throughout the Court.

'What, never?' Melchior demanded, in a loud judicial voice.

'No, never. Never!' admitted the wretched man, wishing he was somewhere else.

So all day long the noise of battle rolled, until the Crown Prosecutor's table, man by man, had fallen in battle about their stricken lord.

For one moment only did the prosecution rally: A young woman was called to say that she was present when the factory manager had locked up the premises for the night and that everything then was safe and sound. To Pomfret's first question she replied, 'No. I wasn't even born in 1956.'

Melchior leant forward, incredulous. 'Not born?' he asked, suspiciously.

'No. Not born.'

He considered that for a moment, puzzled. Then, turning to the witness he enquired sharply, 'Well, were you at the Pig and Whistle Hotel on the Queen's Birthday weekend *this* year?'

She had to admit that she was not, and the jury all gave 'I told you so' nods to one another.

The Crown Prosecutor had the distinct feeling that his watertight, foolproof case was somehow slipping through his fingers, and when he came to his final address he made a valiant effort to restore the balance.

'You may well think, Members of the Jury,' he said, 'that whether or not the Crown witnesses were at the Pig and Whistle Hotel on the Queen's Birthday weekend in 1956 is hardly relevant to the facts in this case—'

'Hardly relevant?' Melchior interrupted him. 'Hardly relevant? Really, Mr Prosecutor, I don't know how you can say such a thing. Defence Counsel has very fairly put the question to every one of the Crown's witnesses and we have all heard their answers. Not one of them was there. Not one. I would advise you not to tell the jury that this is an irrelevant matter, Mr Prosecutor, for I assure you that when I charge them I intend to tell them that it is highly relevant, because . . . ' His voice trailed off as if he was not quite sure why because. At last he added, 'because it is very relevant.'

This reprimand so upset the Crown Prosecutor that he entirely lost his train of thought and delivered the address that he usually made in multiple rape trials, a consequence which caused the jury some confusion, much interest and not a little amusement.

When Melchior finally charged the jury, he left them in no doubt as to what their verdict should be.

'The Crown case depends entirely on the sworn evidence of three witnesses, not one of whom was at the Pig and Whistle Hotel on the Queen's Birthday weekend in 1956. Indeed, Members of the Jury, one of them even admitted that he has never been there. And you might think it very sinister that none of the other witnesses were there either. It is for the Crown to satisfy you beyond reasonable doubt of the guilt of the Accused, but how the Crown could possibly imagine that it has done so without calling at least one witness who was at the Pig and Whistle Hotel on the Queen's Birthday weekend in 1956 is beyond my comprehension. And no doubt beyond yours also,' he added comfortingly.

The jury were out for only four minutes.

'How say you,' asked the Judge's Associate, 'Do you find the Accused Guilty or Not Guilty?'

The Foreman spoke the sweetest words in the world: 'Not Guilty.'

'And is that the verdict of you all?'

'It is,' they assured him.

'Before I discharge the Accused,' Melchior weighed in, 'I would like to apologise to him for the inconvenience and concern which has no doubt been occasioned to him by these proceedings. I trust,' he glowered at the Crown Prosecutor, 'that in future no similar ill-founded and ill-prepared cases will be brought before me for trial. Release the prisoner!'

. . . And I carried young Pomfret back to Chambers in triumph.

By way of celebration I shouted my Reader lunch in the Common Room the next day.

Ordinarily admission to the Common Room is restricted to judges and barristers only, but on one day a week visitors may be invited for lunch.

On this occasion I forgot myself so far as to invite Pomfret's friend, Gerard. For me to have done so, will give you some indication of the relief that I felt at my pupil having come safely through what might have been a mind-scarring ordeal.

By tradition everyone who comes to lunch in the Common Room sits in the next vacant seat. There is no grouping of close friends, no catering for coteries, and the Chief Justice may well find himself sitting next to the newest recruit to the Bar. This helps foster that universal camaraderie which is an essential ingredient of our way of life. When a barrister in Court describes the opponent he is so bitterly fighting as his learned friend, he usually means it.

On this occasion, by chance, who should sit down right beside Pomfret but none other than His Honour Mr Justice Melchior. They nodded, smiled, passed some desultory remarks about the weather, whether Pomfret was enjoying life at the Bar, would you please pass the salt . . .

Then Melchior suddenly asked, somewhat wistfully, a question that had obviously been troubling him overnight: 'I say, Pomfret, there was one matter about that trial which I did not quite understand. Where *is* the Pig and Whistle Hotel?'

Elated, Harry leant forward, directly towards Melchior's face, and replied, 'You are my father, aren't you?'

Melchior who had just placed a forkful of food in his mouth, gave a start, the food went down the wrong way, Melchior went red in the face, blue in the face, purple in the face, coughing in distress.

'What's wrong?' someone asked.

'Quick, hit him on the back,' someone else called.

'Give him a glass of water!'

'Loosen his collar and tie!'

'Send for an ambulance!'

'Phone a doctor!'

'I am a doctor,' that fool of a Gerard volunteered.

'No! Don't! Don't let him touch him!' I cried, but my protestations were lost in the din of agitation and consternation, and Gerard, God help us! began resuscitation procedures.

Harry Pomfret leant over the now prostrate Judge, and asked, 'Are you my father?'

Melchior looked back, eyes wide in distress.

'If you are my father, blink twice,' Harry urged him.

But Melchior did not blink twice, did not even blink once. In fact he never blinked again. Thanks to Gerard's first-aid assistance, Mr Justice Melchior was now on the way to rigor mortis.

FETCH A PRIEST!

The legal profession does not mourn dead judges, barely gives them a thought. Old Melchior was gone and forgotten in less than a week. Everyone was far too interested in guessing who would step into his shoes.

Symons Q.C. ran a book on the hopefuls and the betting was brisk. Eager speculation ran rife as to whether this eminent Counsel, or that, or t'other, would be elevated to the Bench, to inherit old Melchior's Chambers, his library, his Associate, his tipstaff, and the sterling silver tea-service.

Not a damp eye for the deceased. He was important only while he held the whip-hand. Now somebody else was going to be cracking that whip. *Vale* . . . what was his name?

'I was so sure that he must be my father,' Pomfret remarked pensively, 'but he didn't blink when I asked him, so I guess I was mistaken. Who do you think they will appoint in his place?'

'Whom . . . ' I corrected him, *'Whom . . . '*

When I informed Amy that our useless son, on whose education I had squandered a small fortune, had been instrumental in causing the untimely demise of one of Her Majesty's judges, and that I would not be at all surprised if he was charged with manslaughter, she was most indignant.

'You will have to defend him, Dominic,' she asserted hotly, 'I'm sure you can explain to the jury that Gerard was only trying to help.'

'If I defend him, who is going to pay my brief fee?' I growled, endeavouring not to break a tooth on the jam sponge pudding she had cooked as a special treat for me. 'He hasn't a penny to bless himself.'

'You will have to advance Gerard the money and he can repay

you, when he can afford it,' she retorted with all the cool logic of a broody hen protecting her chick.

Of course there was no question of Gerard being charged with manslaughter, or anything else. Doctors are allowed to kill people. The Bar Council even sent him a letter of appreciation for his prompt assistance, and enclosed a cheque by way of honorarium for services rendered. The Bar Council could afford to be prodigal in its protestations of appreciation: more than one of its members suddenly saw, thanks to Gerard's incompetence, a possible golden opportunity for unexpected advancement. Thank you Gerard. Come again as often as you please. We need a young judge-decimating doctor like you around the place.

'Which of the other judges do you think might be my father?' Pomfret asked.

'Try Applebaum,' I replied distractedly, reading a trial brief, and with no time to spare for Pomfret's pursuit of a parent.

'How should I approach him?' my pupil persisted.

'Write him a letter,' I replied flippantly, with an impatient wave of my hand.

I should not have said that. He did:

Dear Judge,

Well, here I am grown up and a barrister at last. Thank you for all those cheques you used to send to my mother. They were a great help. I hope to have the opportunity of meeting you soon, if you wish it.

Your affectionate and respectful son,

Harry.

Mr Justice Applebaum was renowned for his unfailing pleasantness and politeness in court, a very proper judge, scrupulously fair to both sides to a dispute, dispensing justice in a calm and dispassionate manner. With his snow-white hair, fresh clear complexion and chubby pink cheeks, he inspired confidence.

Applebaum was also a family man. His wife was a chronic hypochondriac and he used to hurry home from Court to keep her company, to sympathise with her imaginary illnesses, to fetch and carry for her, to amuse her with anecdotes about what had happened in Court that day. When nothing interesting had occurred, he invented little stories, to make her laugh.

He had three daughters, all married, and they adored him. His grandchildren loved him. His wife idolized him. Yes,

Applebaum was very much a family man. He had been known to confess that his only regret in life was that he had no son.

Not until now, anyway!

The effect of Harry's letter on him was electrifying. He was sitting in his Chambers sipping a morning cup of tea, with a dinner napkin tucked into his waistcoat at the second button, when his tipstaff brought him the letter. Leisurely he opened the envelope . . . A minute later there was tea all over the dinner napkin, all over his waistcoat, all over his striped pants, all over the carpet, and the Crown Derby cup and saucer were shattered remnants at his feet.

It so happened that I was briefed to appear in Applebaum's court that morning, on a Testator's Family Maintenance summons . . .

Henry Nobb had been, to all intents and appearances, a model husband. Only upon his death did his wife discover that he had not been spending all those late evenings working back at the office, but in fact had been dallying with *another woman,* whom he had set up in a comfortable life style on the other side of the Yarra.

So diligently had Henry dallied that his extra-marital liaison had been blessed with a bonny bouncing boy who, at the time of Henry's death, was still at junior school.

The one thing Henry had overlooked was to make some provision for the future welfare of that bonny bouncing boy, and when his Will was read, everything went to his wife and the lawful children of his marriage, and my unfortunate infant client was left out in the cold, to fend for himself.

'I recently had a case like this in front of Mr Justice Applebaum,' I reassured my instructing solicitor, 'and he was quite dogmatic that the policy of the Law is to ensure that a man does not leave his children destitute, whether legitimate or illegitimate.'

My solicitor was relieved to hear me say so.

'We shall win this case on our ear,' I stated confidently, disregarding Amy's dampening observation at breakfast that today Scorpio was in the Seventh Sector, that I had better watch myself.

But when His Honour came into the Practice Court, I was struck by the oddness of his manner. His usual unruffled calm was absent. In fact, he was quite twitchy. When I was only half-way through opening the case, outlining what my client's claim was all about, the Judge testily interrrupted: 'His father didn't make provision for your client in his Will. Why should I?'

Rather taken aback at this uncharacteristic curtness, I attempted to pour oil on troubled waters: 'Y'r Honour has a discretion to vary the provisions of the Will in these cases.'

'I have read the affidavits and I ask you again: Why should I exercise my discretion to vary the Will?' He was trembling with apparent rage. Then he mumbled on, more to himself than to anybody else, 'Children turning up all over the place, writing letters, respectful and affectionate son . . . '

It was at that moment I recalled with dismay my conversation with young Pomfret.

The case was a downhill run all the way. The Judge hardly appeared to hear what I was saying, so obsessed was he by Harry's letter. He rambled on, he uttered little exclamations of indignation, he rolled his eyes and nodded his head so disjointly that I began to fear he might have an apoplectic seizure.

'If I could refer Y'r Honour to the decision in *Re Hobgoblin,'* I urged, in desperation.

'I am well aware of the decision in *Re Hobgoblin,'* Applebaum snapped huffily, 'and it is authority for the fact that I have a discretion to exercise, which I now do, *against* your client.'

'But Y'r Honour—'

'I do not wish to hear Counsel further on this matter.'

'But Y'r Honour—'

'Resume your seat.'

'But—'

'If you persist in this matter, I shall have you arrested for contempt of court!'

I sat.

One does not tempt fate when a judge threatens contempt proceedings. He may fine you, or he may imprison you and leave you to rot in gaol until you purge your contempt, as more than one unfortunate has discovered.

Probably the most famous contempt of court occurred some centuries ago, at a time when the English language was still a hotch-potch of Anglo-Saxon, Latin and Norman-French: A prisoner **ject un brickbat a le Juge que narrowly mist.** The judge immediately ordered the prisoner's right hand **(son manus dexter)** to be amputated and affixed to a gibbet, on which the prisoner himself was then **immediatement hanged in presence de Court.**

Nowadays punishments are rather less severe and courts more tolerant: When a woman witness unwrapped a dead cat from a brown paper parcel and threw it at a Scottish judge, he merely remarked, 'I shall commit you for contempt if you do that again.' Fortunately for her, and for him, she did not have another dead cat with her at the time.

However, I am a natural-born coward and had no intention of seeing whether or not Applebaum would carry out his threat.

'I cannot imagine what could have come over the Judge,' I later apologized to my instructing solicitor. 'Only last week I had an identical case before him, and he made an order in favour of the illegitimate child, without any hassle. I would advise you to appeal,' I added.

'If we do,' my solicitor replied sourly, 'we shall brief other Counsel.'

So there, thanks to the machinations of my pupil, I had probably lost a regular source of income. If this went on much longer, I should soon find myself in queer street.

I did not mention the matter to Harry. It was my own fault, I thought, for facetiously telling him to write a letter to Applebaum.

At least I was not the only one who suffered. Conversation over lunch in the Common Room buzzed about Applebaum's extraordinary behaviour in every case that came before him.

'Y'know,' Macquarie Q.C. said, 'I think the blighter's having a nervous breakdown. He doesn't seem to be able to concentrate—keeps talking about some respectful and affectionate son.'

'He hasn't got a son,' Parsifal remarked, 'only daughters. He's probably gone senile.'

'He kept rambling on about people sending letters to people,' Charleston added, 'which was hardly relevant to the bail application I was making.'

'I was seeking an order for the winding up of an insolvent company,' Hammersmith chimed in, 'and in the middle of it all, he exclaimed that it was probably an attempt at blackmail. I'm sure he wasn't listening to a word I said.'

Clearly the judge had been reduced to a state of great nervous tension, and it would only take a small shove to send him around the twist. And then—

After having given Applebaum J. several days to digest his first letter, Pomfret wrote again:

Dear Father,

When may I expect to meet you? I appreciate that you may prefer to keep our relationship secret, but please insert an advertisement in the Personal and Missing Friends column of the AGE, addressed to 'Pig and Whistle,' nominating a time and place for our meeting.

Respectfully and affectionately,

Your Son,
Harry.

Applebaum was beside himself in agitation. He scrawled out a note and sent his tipstaff forthwith to insert in the *AGE* the reply:

Dear Pig and Whistle, I am not your father.

That, he thought, would be the end of the matter.

Alas . . .

When Applebaum's tipstaff (the soul of discretion) filled out the usual requisite form in the *AGE* office, one of those terse young ladies whose working hours comprise the speed-reading of thousands upon thousands of classified advertisements, asked, 'By whom is this being inserted? You have to write that on the form.'

The tipstaff accordingly added, laboriously: 'His . . . Honour . . . Mr . . . Justice . . . Applebaum . . . is . . .' He paused, not certain whether to continue '. . . the sender of this message', or '. . . the inserter of this advertisement'.

The young lady, moving from person to person along the counter, returned.

'You have put it in the wrong place. You must write that at the top.'

Applebaum's tipstaff did as directed, paid the price of the advertisement, and made his way back to the Supreme Court.

Unfortunately, he forgot to cross out the words he had added to the bottom of the message. Next morning, those who perused the Personal and Missing Friends column were surprised to read:

Dear Pig and Whistle. I am not your father. His Honour Mr Justice Applebaum is.

Members of the legal profession are great readers of the *AGE,* from the first page to the last, and by 9.15 a.m. the telephones between solicitors' offices were running hot, the corridors in Barristers' Chambers were agog with laughing gossip, the Chief Justice and the Senior Puisne Judge were closeted in urgent conference, and altogether the entire legal fraternity was either squirming with embarrassment or rocking with laughter.

Applebaum sat at the desk in his Chambers, the *AGE* opened at page 47, in a state of complete shock and dismay. When he went into court he was greeted with broad grins and the morning's proceedings were enlivened by covert sniggers and sly, smiling eyes. His nerves were at breaking point. He completely lost track of what he was doing, what he was saying, what the case was all about. Finally he could stand the strain no longer, and just before midday he quit.

'All stand!' bellowed his tipstaff. 'This Honourable Court stands adjourned until 10-30 o'clock tomorrow morning. God save the Queen!'

Applebaum beat an ungainly retreat, almost at a run, and went to sit in his Chambers, his head in his hands.

During the afternoon the Chief Justice sent for him. When Applebaum arrived, the great man waved him to a chair. There was a short embarrassed silence. The Chief Justice walked to a window and looked out at the traffic in the street below. Applebaum gazed despairingly at the Chief Justice's back. Why is it, he thought distractedly to himself, that Chief Justices are always little fat roley-poley men, with bald heads?

'I say, Applebaum,' said the Chief Justice, suddenly turning around, '*whose* father are you?'

Mr Justice Applebaum did not reply. He just burst into tears.

For the rest of that afternoon he remained in his Chambers, not moving, staring at the bookcases surrounding him. Being pompous is an occupational hazard of a judge's life, and when he suddenly finds himself an object of merriment, the butt of jokes of the entire legal profession, it is a sad, cruel blow to an old man.

Meanwhile his wife's very best friend had telephoned her and enquired whether she had read the Personal and Missing Friends column on page 47 of this morning's *AGE?* The very best friends of each of his daughters had done as much for them.

When Applebaum arrived home he was greeted by his spouse

and three children sitting there in a row, in silence, looking accusingly at him with as much mercy in their hearts as a French Revolutionary Committee of Public Safety.

He went to speak, could find no words, and went straight to bed, unfed, unwashed, unforgiven.

Next morning he arose betimes, before dawn, and made his way, in a state of utter desolation, to the Supreme Court.

The Supreme Court at Melbourne occupies half a city block. It is an imposing edifice in sandstone, erected around the four sides of a square, with a large interior bluestone cobbled courtyard. Built in the 1880's on the affluence afforded by the gold-diggings at Bendigo and Ballarat, it is a shrine to the majesty of the law. The courts are immense, with ceilings some thirty feet or more high, decorated with cornices and friezes hand-painted by Italian craftsmen in pastel shades and gold leaf.

In each court the Judge sits enthroned on the Bench, backed by richly polished deep-red wood panelling, high above those lesser beings down below in the well of the court. Soaring above his head and supported by stout rounded timber pillars is a grand, ornate canopy. Even the long Bar table, where the barristers sit, is elaborately hand-carved, and worth a fortune in this day and age. The jury box, the witness box, the panelled walls, the dock where the Accused is imprisoned during a trial, the public gallery high in the air at the back of the court and fronted with ornamental cast-iron lacework: all these are of an opulence undreamed of by latter-day architects.

At the entrance to the Courts stands an imposing portico, an arcade of Doric columns below, supporting an arcade of Ionic columns above. Above this portico sits the bronze statue of Justice, a pair of scales in one hand, a sword in the other. Unlike almost all other statues of Justice in the world, this imposing figure is not blindfolded. There she sits, contemplating the mere mortals in the streets below, and facing directly towards Barristers' Chambers. As learned Counsel sit at their desks preparing their briefs, writing their Opinions, this lady peers thoughtfully through their windows and over their shoulder. And as their clients sit there in conference trying to make up their mind what to tell their Counsel and what to conceal, they are outfaced by this stern lady, staring at them, daring them to come over the road and into her Courts and not tell the truth, the whole truth and nothing but the truth, so help me God. There through the ages she sits impassive, a symbol of power, punishment and protection.

On that auspicious morning, early wanderers and workers were startled to see, high in the air and sitting on the lap of the Statue of Justice, cradled in her arms and cuddled against her motherly bosom, a solitary figure clad in scarlet and ermine, wearing a full-bottomed wig, and weeping.

By the time I arrived at Chambers, a large crowd had gathered. Someone had fetched an extension ladder and placed it up against the top of the portico, but when a policeman had climbed up, Applebaum cried, 'Go away! Go away!' with such vehemence that the policeman had deemed it prudent to climb down again, lest the judge should do himself a mischief.

Somehow escaped from their solicitors' offices, a group of young articled clerks had positioned themselves on the opposite side of the road and were by now chanting in unison, 'Jump! Jump! Jump! Jump! Jump! Jump! Jump! Jump! . . . '

'Fetch a priest,' suggested the Senior Partner of the legal firm Morgenstein, Eisenstein, Frankenstein and Smith.

'I am a priest,' one of the crowd said. There always is a priest on the spot at times like this. It is common knowledge that they prowl around the city waiting for someone to threaten to jump off a building.

But when the policeman suggested that this priest should climb the ladder and talk to Applebaum, the priest declined.

'I have acrophobia,' he said.

The policeman retreated a step.

'Is it infectious?' he enquired.

'Acrophobia is a fear of heights,' the priest explained, 'I couldn't possibly climb the ladder.'

At this moment young Pomfret arrived. Taking in the scene at a glance, he pushed his way towards the policeman.

'I will go up,' he offered, and not waiting for a yea or nay, he began to climb. Up, up he went until he was near enough to be heard by Applebaum, who had watched his ascent, numbly, distractedly, apprehensively.

'Father! Father!' Pomfret called. 'I am your son, Harry.'

For Mr Justice Applebaum, this was the final straw.

He jumped.

Cuddled against her motherly bosom

THE HAZARDS OF A ROYAL AND ANCIENT GAME

After the funeral and in a burst of remorse, the late Mr Justice Applebaum's tipstaff told me, in the very strictest confidence, the full story of how a misunderstanding at the *AGE* office had resulted in the appearance of that unfortunate advertisement in the Personal and Missing Friends column. Of course I told Pomfret.

'Then he was not my father, after all,' he commented.

'Decidedly not,' I assured him.

'Oh well,' he sighed. Then brightening: 'Who do you think they will appoint in his place?'

'*Whom* . . . ' I corrected him, '*Whom* . . . '

When a young man is first called to the Bar, he is required for a period to read with a Master, another experienced barrister of some years calling, who points the nose of this fledgling in the right direction, tutors him on Court etiquette and legal ethics, advises him how to prepare and present his cases, and assumes responsibility for the behaviour, conformity and diligence of this newcomer.

Once his apprenticeship is finished and the now fully-feathered barrister is thrown out of the nest and into the cold cruel world of kill or be killed, he will thereafter be quite alone, must stand on his own two feet. If he is successful, solicitors will send him briefs. If he fails, he must throw himself over the edge of one of those charming bridges which cross and criss-cross the River Yarra, and drown.

Unlike a solicitor, a barrister cannot enter into a partnership, no matter how eminent a Q.C. he may one day become. He is forever solitary. Yet, in that solitude, there is a lively fellowship among members of the Bar. No Counsel who goes to another to seek help, or advice, or to discuss a difficult case, is ever turned away. Indeed, the barrister whose help or advice is sought will drop everything to assist his adversary. It is a commonplace of the Bar that men who have day after day fought tooth and nail against one another, will just as readily move heaven and earth to help the same opponent whose blood they so joyfully spilled yesterday. This makes for a very close bond between members of the Bar. They are probably the most tightly-knit group in the community.

But when a young man first arrives, and while he is still a Reader, he is very much a protected species, labelled 'Handle with Care'.

Because of our Master and Slave relationship, I felt myself personally responsible for Harry Pomfret's inept approach to old Applebaum, and the judge's premature going to God. *Mea culpa.* So I decided that I must take an active part in Pomfret's search for a sire, rather than abandon him to his own devices.

'Did your mother leave anything when she died?' I asked him, 'anything which might provide a clue as to the identity of your father?'

'There was a photograph,' he responded, taking out his wallet and extracting a small snapshot. He handed it to me, questioningly.

Half of the photograph had been cut off. What was left showed an attractive young woman, sitting on the grass, and around her shoulder was a man's arm. The man on the other end of that arm had been carefully snipped away with scissors.

I turned the photograph over. Handwritten on the reverse were the remnants:

rthday
956

'What do you think?' Pomfret asked.

'I think that what was originally written there could well have been *Queen's Birthday 1956.*'

'And that is my father's arm?'

'Very probably.'

I looked again at the snapshot. The only thing of significance to be noted on that arm, on that hand, was that the man was wearing a signet ring. And in 1956 this was most unusual.

Nowadays lots of young men wear rings, wedding rings, signet rings, fancy rings set with precious and semi-precious stones or just pieces of glass. They also wear chains around their necks, and beads, and ear-rings. They even have their ears pierced and wear sleepers. I really can't think what the world is coming to. Rings on their fingers—perhaps even bells on their toes, for all I know.

In 1956 they would have been kicked to death. In those days, the most daring would not have been seen in public sporting anything more than a plain gold signet ring, with his initials engraved. Even then, he usually had to explain it away as a twenty-first birthday present or a gift from his wife.

Suddenly I remembered: Mr Justice Kneebone used to wear a signet ring! He was then an up-and-coming barrister, and when he wanted to emphasize a point in an address to a jury, he would rap on the Bar table with this ring and the twelve jurors would jump all at once, as if they had been shot. Not only did he startle the jury but he used to startle drowsy judges as well, not to mention us other barristers.

I looked carefully at the photograph. 'I have good reason to believe,' I remarked to my pupil, 'that your father is none other than Sir Frederick Kneebone.'

Kneebone was a very popular judge, a tremendous golfer, and a man with a lively sense of humour. He had received a knighthood in the last New Year's Honours list and was now at the prime of his life, as happy as a skylark. Everything was going his way.

He might not be altogether pleased, I thought, to find some youthful indiscretion suddenly dumped on his doorstep, in a basket.

'How should I ask him?' Pomfret queried.

'Do nothing,' I replied hastily. 'Do nothing! I will think of a way.'

I was not at leisure to give further thought to the matter just then, because one of my most fervent admirers among solicitors had just arrived, bringing his client to an urgent conference, for a trial that was about to begin.

It was imperative that I should be on my toes for this trial. That very morning, as Amy presided at the kitchen sink, scouring the encrusted black off the pot in which she had burnt my breakfast, bless her, she had confided to me in awed tones,

'Today, Leo is in conflict with Capricorn. For you, this is a day of violence.'

I looked apprehensively at the client for whom I was to appear. Mr Bargery was indeed a very big man, with thick hands. I must make sure I won his case for him.

Auguste Bargery was a spec-builder who had erected a house for sale on a vacant block of land which he had bought, as they say, dirt cheap. Unfortunately for Mr Bargery, he failed to have the land surveyed before commencing to build, and in fact had erected the house on the block next door.

This block next door was owned by Mr and Mrs Giuseppe DiMaggio, ex-Calabrians now trying to make a new life for themselves in their adopted country. They too had bought their block very cheaply and hoped one day to build a dream house on it. Those expectations were continually delayed by reason of the fact that Mrs DiMaggio was continually expecting. No sooner was she delivered of one bambino that she was pregnant with the next.

Every so often Mr and Mrs and all the little DiMaggios would go for a Sunday drive to inspect their block, dream their dreams, pick blackberries and collect mushrooms.

Imagine their surprise when they arrived one Sunday afternoon to find a double-fronted brick veneer villa sitting in the middle of their land. After much excited discussion and speculation, Mr DiMaggio forced a window and inspected the inside. It was a verra nice-a house, he called out to his wife, much-a better than the one they were renting—and even the light-a fittings and-a curtains had been installed.

Without more ado they hurried home, summoned all their numerous friends and relations, and soon a convoy of cars laden with household furniture and effects (and a crateful of chooks) was en route. Nothing remained to be done but to change the locks, and Mrs DiMaggio's sister's husband's father's uncle's best friend happened to be a locksmith.

When Auguste Bargery arrived on the Monday morning to erect a FOR SALE sign, he was somewhat taken aback.

The DiMaggios refused to vacate, so Mr Bargery called a policeman. But when Mr DiMaggio, urged on by Mrs DiMaggio's loud excited Italian shrieking, produced a Certificate of Title, the policeman confessed there was nothing he could do about it.

So Mr Bargery's solicitor issued a Supreme Court writ, and now I was briefed to appear on his behalf.

'You have a problem,' I apologetically tried to explain to my outraged client, 'at law the ownership of land includes everything attached to it, the trees, the shrubs, the flowers—and the house. By building the house on the DiMaggio's land, it has become their property.'

He was astounded.

'Not only that,' I continued dolefully, 'but every fixture in the house becomes part of the land. This includes the bath, the built-in wardrobes, the power-points—' I shook my head in a show of sad resignation.

Mr Bargery shook his head too. For one awful minute I thought he was going to attack me and I recalled vividly Amy's dire warning that Leo was today in conflict with Capricorn, that I must beware of violence.

'I didn't make the law,' I explained hastily, 'and I can't change it either. Of course,' I went on soothingly, 'the lamp-shades and the curtains aren't fixtures, so they can't keep those . . . '

As he again looked as if he might attack me, I hurriedly scooped back into their folder all the plans, diagrams, specifications and photographs that he had brought, and added, 'I will do my best for you, of course. Now your solicitor will take you over to the Court. I will do my best, Mr Bargery, I will do my best.'

In my alarm, together with the photographs of internal and external views of the disputed dwelling house, I also mistakenly swept into the folder the photograph of Pomfret's mother.

'You had better come and watch, and you might learn something,' I told Pomfret as I left Chambers, my heart in my boots, which is a very common feeling among barristers when they know they have to fight a losing battle, with no possible hope of winning. Rather like the Blessed Saint Sebastian, stuck full of arrows.

The trial was before Sir Frederick Kneebone himself and, by way of putting up some sort of a show in a hopeless cause, I attempted to swamp him with documents.

'I tender the plans of the dwelling-house,' I said firmly.

'Exhibit A,' he rejoined.
'And the specifications.'
'Exhibit B.'
'And the working drawings.'
'Exhibit C.'
'And photographs of the house.'
'Exhibit D . . .' He began to inspect these disinterestedly when suddenly he stopped, his eye caught by a very *non sequitur* snapshot. He appeared so engrossed in perusing this photograph, looking first at the front of it, then at the back, that I paused.
Finally he glanced down at me and said, 'There is an exhibit here that I do not quite understand.' And he held it up for my inspection.
'My apologies, Y'r Honour, it must have got in there by mistake,' I assured him, and then, seizing opportunity by the forelock, added nonchalantly, 'It is a photograph of m' learned Reader's mother, taken in . . . taken in . . . '
'1956, it seems to say on the back,' Kneebone prompted me, with some apparent interest.
'Just so, 1956. I understand at the Pig and Whistle Hotel, Y'r Honour, on the Queen's Birthday 1956, Y'r Honour.'
At this gratuitous information, Kneebone appeared quite surprised, but merely commented, 'Well, I don't think that's very relevant to the matters in question in this action, y'know.'
As he was about to pass the photograph to his Associate, to pass to his tipstaff, to pass to my instructing solicitor, to pass to me, he gazed at it again, and commented, 'I used to wear a ring like that.' And looking down at Pomfret, who was seated behind me, he added, 'That is your pupil, isn't it?'
'Yes, Y'r Honour, indeed. Mr Harry Pomfret.'
Kneebone looked searchingly at Harry for a moment, then smiled encouragingly. 'You have chosen a very experienced and skilful Master to read with, Mr Pomfret.'
That did not stop me from losing the case, though. As we left the Court I consoled my client, 'Well, at least you get back the light fittings and the curtains.'
'What are the good of the light fittings and the curtains, without the house?' he churlishly replied.
They say misfortunes never come singly. The very next day the very same solicitor briefed me to appear in another trial in

the very same court before the very same judge, and the defendant's case was just as hopeless: The Commissioner of Probate Duties was suing a young widow for the death duties on her deceased husband's estate, and she just refused to pay.

'She can't win,' I assured my instructing solicitor, 'Incurring my exorbitant brief fee to appear on her behalf is only going to increase the debt around her neck.'

'What should I do?' the solicitor asked.

'Give the brief to my Reader,' I replied. 'It will be good experience for him, and he certainly can't do any harm, because the widow is going to lose the case anyway. At least you won't have to pay very much for him to appear.'

And so Harry Pomfret was briefed in the action.

The defendant widow had, at the age of twenty-two years, married a bridegroom of eighty-four. After six weeks' effort he died, leaving her sole beneficiary of a very considerable estate.

'When one door closes, another opens,' the distraught young widow had most stoically observed, but her stoic philosophy had received a nasty jolt when the Commissioner of Probate Duties had jumped in for his chop.

'Never!' she had declared 'Never! He left all his money to me and I'm going to keep it.' Then she tactfully added, 'That was the wish of my dear, dead husband, and I don't intend him to be disappointed.'

When her solicitor brought her to my Chambers for a conference with young Pomfret, she seemed quite put out.

'You don't look like a very good barrister, to me,' she observed.

'I'm not,' he admitted.

She scrutinized him carefully, then said, 'All right. I'll tell you what you have to do to win this case.'

. . . I left them to it.

The Court was practically empty. Nobody was very interested in an action for debt brought by the Commissioner of Probate Duties. The only spectators in that great cavernous Courtroom were three vagrants who had come in out of the rain, and sat huddled in the middle of the front row of the public gallery.

Sir Frederick Kneebone listened gravely as Counsel appearing for the Commissioner of Probate Duties outlined his case, called formal evidence, and then announced, 'That is the case for the plaintiff, if Y'r Honour pleases.'

Then His Honour looked at Harry, somewhat indulgently, smiling that benign smile with which judges watch drowning men clutch at straws.

'Yes?' he enquired, 'What has your client to say to all this, Mr Pomfret?'

'If Y'r Honour pleases,' Harry began (good boy, good boy), 'the defendant denies the debt.'

'Really?' Kneebone purred.

'She asserts that the deceased died possessed of no assets.'

'Really?' Kneebone purred on. 'But what about all those broad acres, these blocks of flats, this city office building? . . . and the yacht . . . and the Rolls Royce . . . not to mention all those shares and other gilt-edged securities that appear in the Probate Inventory. Does she deny that at the time of the deceased's death they were all registered in his name?'

'No, Y'r Honour,' Harry stoutly continued, 'but she says that they were only held by the deceased in trust for her and on her behalf.'

'Really?' Kneebone purred and purred.

'Before his death the deceased made a gift to my client of all his worldly goods.'

'Really? And what was the reason for such generosity?' Kneebone's smile had become almost a death's head grin.

'It was a gift made in consideration of marriage, Y'r Honour, and evidenced in writing.'

'Really?' . . . purr . . . purr.

The three vagrants, observing such amiability on the part of the judge, smiled happily at one another.

But the Judge's amiability was even further increased when Harry called the defendant to the witness box, to give evidence. King Solomon himself would have described her as comely. She was dressed for the occasion in widow's weeds comprising a very, very tight black sheath dress which left little to the imagination and reassured everybody that at least the deceased died happy.

Kneebone, who had been a bit of a lady's man in his day, began to wonder whether he might not be able to bend the law a little, just a little, to find in favour of the defendant. He gazed thoughtfully at her as she stood there taking the oath, fluttering her wide eyes which resembled nothing so much as the eyes of those three dogs in the Hans Christian Andersen fairy tale of the Tinder Box.

Having announced her name and address and stated that her occupation was widow, the witness looked expectantly at Harry, hoping he would remember the questions she had told him to ask.

'Were you,' he began, 'married to the deceased according to the rites of the Church of England?'

'I was,' she responded, fluttering her eyes the size of soup spoons.

'Who married you?'

'The Archbishop of Melbourne, himself.' The eyes like soup spoons widened to eyes the size of teacups.

'And during the course of that ceremony did the deceased say anything to you?'

'Yes,' the eyes like teacups widened to eyes the size of saucers, 'He said: *With this ring I thee wed, with my body I thee worship and with all my worldly goods I thee endow*. That's what he said.'

'Really?' Mr Justice Kneebone was very impressed.

Harry continued his examination-in-chief: 'Those were his exact words—*with all my worldly goods I thee endow?*'

'His very words.' The eyes like saucers rounded to eyes the size of bread-and-butter plates.

'And after the ceremony, did you and the bridegroom go to the vestry and there sign a printed document?' Harry triumphantly waved in the air the original Marriage Certificate.

'We did,' she replied.

'I tender the Marriage Certificate, Y'r Honour,' Harry said. The three vagrants bent forward over the front rail of the public gallery, craning to read it from a distance, and then whispered excitedly together.

'That will be . . . Exhibit A,' intoned Kneebone, and his Associate marked it accordingly.

'And did you sign that document in the presence of witnesses?' Harry pursued the point.

'Yes.' Now the eyes widened to the size of soup coupes.

'And did those witnesses also sign the document?'

'They did.' Now the size of dinner plates.

'I intend to call those witnesses, Y'r Honour,' Harry announced to the judge, who smiled beneficently.

A pity he was not of the True Faith

'During the remaining six weeks of his life, did the deceased perfect that gift and transfer all his assets to you?'

'No,' she dabbed her wide, wide, innocent, fluttering eyes with a pretty lace handkerchief.

The three empathetic vagrants also wiped the tears from their eyes.

'Was there any discussion about him doing so?'

'Yes, on numerous occasions I asked him when he was going to make a formal transfer to me of all the worldly goods with which he had me endowed.'

'Was the deceased offended by these remarks?'

'No, he was very happy.'

'How do you know?'

'He laughed.'

At which the three vagrants also smiled happily.

As the witness left the box and wiggled her way back to her place in the Court, His Honour watched her approvingly.

'Call the Anglican Archbishop of Melbourne,' Harry requested.

The Judge's tipstaff bustled out of Court and his voice could be heard echoing and re-echoing along the high vaulted corridors: 'The Archbishop of Melbourne! . . . The Archbishop of Melbourne! . . . The Archbishop of Melbourne! . . .'

There was a slight delay. The Archbishop was in the Gents.

When His Grace finally entered, swishing very ecclesiastically, his gold pectoral crucifix swinging to and fro across his purple stock, the three vagrants automatically crossed themselves, in an outburst of religious fervour.

The Archbishop took the oath. There is always something slightly ridiculous about bishops and archbishops being required to swear to tell the truth, the whole truth and nothing but the truth. The mind boggles at the possibility of them being guilty of wilful and corrupt perjury. Especially this Archbishop. He cut a very impressive figure . . . A pity he was not of the True Faith.

Yes, His Grace had performed the wedding ceremony, and he identified his signature on Exhibit A. The marriage, he said, had been solemnized according to the General Rubricks of the King James Version of the Book of Common Prayer, and from one of the voluminous pockets of his frock coat he produced a copy of the book in question.

'Exhibit B,' Kneebone intoned.

'And do the words *will all my worldly goods I thee endow* form part of that ceremony and are they spoken by the groom?'

'Indeed they do and they are.'

'And does the Marriage Certificate signed by the deceased specifically acknowledge that the marriage was solemnized according to the rites of the Church of England?'

'It does.'

By way of further conclusive evidence, Harry called Miss Layback and Mr Bestfoote-Forward, both of whom were ready to corroborate anything and everything.

After that, the case was a lay-down *misere*. Sir Frederick had no difficulty in holding that the deceased had orally and in a public place, to wit, a church, entered into a legally binding contract with his widow, to wit, the defendant, which contract had been reduced to writing, to wit, Exhibit A, and signed in the presence of witnesses, to wit, Miss Layback and Mr Bestfoote-Forward. He also held that such contract was deemed by its premises to incorporate the terms and conditions appearing in Exhibit B, to wit, the King James Version of the Book of Common Prayer. Accordingly all assets of the deceased had thereupon passed to the Widow, and at the time of the deceased's death he was a pauper, with no Estate upon which Probate duties could be payable. There would be judgment for the defendant widow, whose costs must be paid by the plaintiff.

Whereupon the Commissioner of Probate Duties skulked off with his tail between his legs, amid prolonged and tumultuous applause from the three vagrants.

'Order!' demanded Kneebone, banging the Bench with his gavel, 'or I shall clear the Court!' and he glared savagely around the vast empty spaces of the vast empty courtroom, vacant save for the three tiny specks huddled together in the middle of the front row of the public gallery.

Having restored order, the learned Judge then so far forgot himself as to lean forward across the Bench and say to Harry Pomfret, 'Jolly well done, my boy.'

It had stopped raining. The three vagrants stood, made their way to the aisle, reverently genuflected to His Honour and left.

'He called me *his boy*!' Harry reported excitedly to me. 'He *must* be my father.'

'We can soon put that to the test,' I assured him.

'How?'

'Every Sunday afternoon Sir Fredererick plays golf at the Royal Melbourne. He has a regular booking for 2.30.'

Pomfret looked puzzled.

I went on, 'I shall book us in for 2.15. He will easily catch us up. He plays to a handicap of 4, you know. When he does catch us up, he will say Good Afternoon and exchange a few words. We shall ask him then.'

'Do you think he won't mind?' Pomfret anxiously wondered.

'If he does, the worst he can do is hit you over the head with a niblick,' I told him. 'Don't worry. Just leave it all to me.'

And so it came to pass.

We hit off at 2.15. Sir Frederick and his partner hit off at 2.30. By 3 o'clock they were hard on our heels.

'I say, Dominic, d'you mind if we play through you chaps?' Kneebone called.

We stood politely aside, succintly indicating tacit acceptance of the long-established legal principle that a Supreme court judge's slightest whim is our command.

Sir Frederick was gracious: 'That was a jolly nice photo of y'r mother, young Pomfret, the other day. Jolly nice.'

Looking around to make sure there was nobody else within earshot, I took opportunity of the occasion to remark, 'We thought *you* might be his father.'

Kneebone, halfway through a swing with a four-iron, stood suddenly transfixed, like a classical Greek marble.

'What's that?' he asked.

'We have reason to believe that Pomfret's father is a judge, and we thought it might be you,' I repeated, in for a penny, in for a pound.

There was a moment's pause, then Kneebone laughed loudly. 'Afraid not, old chap. Sorry I can't oblige.' He looked at Pomfret. 'Would be delighted if I was. You seem a fine young fellow. But afraid not, afraid not.'

He hit off, but before continuing on his way, added, again laughing, 'I say, that means one of my very respectable brother

Judges has a skeleton in his closet.' Hastily he reassured Harry, 'No offence of course. But very droll, very.'

And he went off after his ball.

As we watched him strolling down the fairway Pomfret remarked, 'I like him. I really like him. I wish he were my father.'

'Well there's now no doubt that he is not,' I replied. 'But at least that eliminates one of the suspects.'

Pomfret stationed himself beside his golf-ball, made sure his feet were firmly positioned, his back and arms were straight, his eye was on the ball. Then taking a steady clean swing, he drove the ball with an accuracy that any pro might have envied. The ball went up, up in a graceful arc high in the air, straight along the fairway.

I watched its flight.

'Fore!' I suddenly shouted in alarm.

'Fore!' yelled Harry.

'Fore!' I shouted again, in even greater alarm.

'Fore!' yelled Harry at the top of his voice.

Sir Frederick, hearing our calls, turned back to see whatever was untoward, just in time to be struck by Harry's golfball in the left temple and killed outright.

'I wonder,' Pomfret pondered, as a few moments later we stood gazing down at the judicial corpse, 'I wonder who they will appoint in his place.'

'*Whom* . . .' I corrected him, '*Whom* . . .'

NOT WITH MY DAUGHTER, YOU DON'T

Then Harry Pomfret fell in love.

Harry Pomfret fell in love with a judge's daughter.

Harry Pomfret fell in love with the daughter of His Honour Mr Justice Philanderer. Unfortunately Mr Justice Philanderer was one of the judges on my list of suspects.

When I first saw Harry with his *inamorata*, I got a terrible shock. She had fair wavy hair—so did her father, and so did Harry. She had pale grey eyes—her father likewise; Harry too. Together she and Harry looked like brother and sister. I began to become quite perturbed. It was all too much of a coincidence.

What made it more embarrassing was the fact that George Philanderer and I were first cousins. His career had outstripped mine, of course, so that while I still wore the stuff gown of the run-of-the-mill barrister, George had exchanged his for the silk gown of a Queen's Counsel and then risen to the scarlet and ermine of one of Her Majesty's Supreme Court judges.

When we were young I had not seen much of George. We went to different schools. He was at Xavier, where the Jesuit Fathers carefully groomed him for the brilliant career which lay before him. Meanwhile, under the watchful eyes of the Christian Brothers, I was obliged to play football every spare minute of the morning, noon and night, in order to rid my mind of impure thoughts and by way of expiation for the original sin which hung around my neck like an albatross. Naturally, George left school knowing he was a very superior person, whereas the Christian Brothers' pupils all graduated with a delicious guilt complex. The certain knowledge that we were unredeemable miserable sinners was to remain with us for the rest of our lives.

It was only when we were both at University that I really got to know Philanderer, and then we became close friends. We played in the same football team, the same cricket team, and we joined forces in a gallant attempt to seduce the entire female population of the Arts Faculty. Together we undertook the mandatory undergraduate pilgrimage of those days, drinking one glass of beer in every hotel between the G.P.O. and the University. By the time we arrived back at the Law School, George was paralytic.

The other students used to call us the Terrible Twins. I suppose there was some family resemblance—people said we looked alike but I could never see it—and we were always together. Even after we left the University, and were later both called to the Bar, we still continued to hell-rake a little, and several times just missed being locked up in the cells overnight for being drunk and disorderly.

It was only when we married and settled down that we drifted apart. From about the time Gerard was born, I saw less and less of George Philanderer. He and his wife moved in social circles much more grand than Amy and I could aspire to, so in the end, as the years passed, we became almost strangers. If we had not regularly bumped into one another in Chambers and in the Law Courts, our acquaintance would have entirely ceased. After he was elevated to the Bench, the only occasions we ever saw one another was when I was briefed to appear in a trial before him.

But it's a small world. Here I was, with a pupil who was the spitting image of Mr Justice Philanderer when young, and who had fallen in love with his daughter Clare! Not that I could blame Harry—Clare was a devilish pretty girl. I had not seen her often over the last few years, only at the occasional family weddings and funerals, and was surprised, and delighted, to see how she had blossomed into such an attractive young woman. She always called me Uncle, but our relationship was so distant that it was no more than a courtesy title.

I had noticed her with Harry on several occasions, and had paid no real attention, assuming it was just a platonic friendship. Of couse, if I had been a year or two younger I would have recognized that there is no such thing: The very idea of platonic friendship is a fantasy of middle-age onwards, sheer wishful thinking. I first realised that Harry had actually fallen in love with Clare when I saw them dancing together at a society ball in the Great Hall of the Arts Centre.

The City of Melbourne boasts an art collection unrivalled in any of the other States of Australia. At the turn of the century one Alfred Felton left to the Art Gallery a handsome bequest—not money, but shares in a company. The dividends from these shares were to be used for the purchase of works of art. It was a handsome gift, but more handsome than the late Mr Felton anticipated. The company produced and sold pharmaceutical products. Nobody in 1904 could have anticipated the twentieth century explosion in the pharmaceutical market. There was an enormous increase in the value of shares and of the dividends derived therefrom. So great did the income from this bequest become that the Art Gallery acquired a collection of all major artists—Rembrandt, Goya, Velasquez, Gainsborough, Boucher, Reynolds—such a valuable collection that it became an embarrassment. The bequest provided only for the purchase of works of art: there was no money for their proper housing, no money to pay the Gallery attendants. For years many of these *objets d'art* languished in dungeons, hidden away from public view.

Finally, a building suitable for housing these treasures was erected. The exterior of this building is almost forbidding, a fortress reminiscent of some Bastille, unrelieved by any windows, a solid bluestone fortress, fronted by a moat. But once inside, there are delights to enchant the mind and the soul, and it seems that almost every third exhibit is labelled *Felton Bequest*, all splendidly displayed, and appropriately lighted. Not only the art connoisseurs throng to marvel at these wonders, but the man on the Clapham omnibus and the ladies from Moonee Ponds also come to gaze in awe and admiration.

Now, in the centre of this grand edifice stands a Great Hall, mediaeval in architecture and conception, with a ceiling high above constructed of thousands upon thousands of pieces of stained glass, a vast window through which the daylight shines in a blazing kaleidoscope of dazzling colour. People often lie down on the floor, the more properly to view this overhead masterpiece, and art lovers have to be careful not to tread on somebody's head.

The Great Hall is frequently used for chamber music recitals, oratorio, and the like, and during the entr'acte one can wander through the antechambers, admiring here an oil by Turner, there a Persian carpet of great antiquity, water colours by Australian artists, and, in an adjacent courtyard, the larger than life-size bronzes of Henry Moore and Rodin . . .

Amy and I attended a formal ball in the Great Hall, arranged by the Friends of the Victorian Society of the Arts and Sciences, and it was an occasion of considerable excitement and glamour. And so it should have been, at $130.00 a head. Dress was strictly formal—black tie and dinner suit for the men, haute-couture ball gowns for the women. Everywhere the glitter of precious stones, clustered at the throat, falling low over the bosom, clasped in the hair, twisted around the arms, pinned to the shoulder, indicated that there had been a sustained rush on the safety-boxes of many a bank's strong-room.

The Great Hall was over-brightly lighted, with additional spotlights in the arched alcoves high above, shining down on the social set at play. The champagne was flowing and everywhere a bright buzz of conversation and laughter rose above the music. For the dancing, two bands alternated: one playing that modern sort of dance music, the other, a baroque chamber group, playing old-time for the more mature.

Amy and I stood a while, chatting to a neurologist and an orthopaedic surgeon from St Francis Xavier Cabrini Hospital, and their wives. We watched the young people on the dance floor, gyrating their torsos, wiggling their behinds, waggling their arms, not touching, just gazing vacantly into space.

'I imagine,' remarked the orthopaedic surgeon reflectively, 'that there will be more than a few slipped discs before the evening is out.'

'And probably a few cerebral episodes,' muttered the neurologist, looking around at the champagne flowing like water. 'There is nothing like an overdose of alcohol in the aged to bring on a stroke.'

The music stopped and the young people drifted from the dance floor. Then the baroque chamber group took the place of the modern music-makers. Whereupon, those other couples, who had left their progeny in the care of baby-sitters for the evening, put down their champagne glasses and edged towards the parquetry. A fox-trot was heard, slow-slow-fast-fast-slow, and again the dance floor was thronged. I noticed Gerard among the dancers, with a very pretty girl. 'Where does he find them all?' I thought, 'As a doctor he's a dead-loss, but as a gigolo he'd be a roaring success.' Then the chamber group began to play a waltz, an old-fashioned Viennese one-two-three-one-two-three, and now the ball gowns were spinning, the girls held firmly and competently on the arms of their dinner-suited companions.

'I didn't realize anybody knew how to waltz nowadays,' I observed, with some surprise.

'Well, they all seem to know,' Amy replied, 'though I've no idea where they learnt.'

As we stood watching the whirling dancers, my attention was irresistibly drawn to a remarkable couple, outstanding even in that brilliantly dressed throng. Both fair-haired, and so strikingly alike, they stood out from the multitude as they were swept along by the circular waltz, both leaning slightly backwards as they revolved, smiling at one another. The attention of the electricians in the alcoves above was apparently also caught, and all their spotlights gradually converged on this young couple, lighting up more intensely the darkness of his black dinner suit and her sweeping white satin ball-gown. In the battery of powerful arc lights, the fair hair of each of them radiated an almost golden hue.

Amy tugged my sleeve. 'Dominic, isn't that George Philanderer's daughter?' she asked rhetorically, 'And who's that young man she's dancing with?'

'That young man,' I answered grimly, 'is my pupil, Harry Pomfret.'

'Such a handsome young man,' Amy remarked. 'They make a splendid couple.'

Harry and the Judge's daughter danced on and on, eyes only for one another, obviously head over heels in love. All the world loves a lover, and instinctively every eye was drawn towards them. Gradually, and for no apparent reason, the other dancers fell out, couple by couple, until finally there were only Harry and the Philanderer girl left on the floor, completely unaware that they had become the focus of so much attention.

The baroque chamber group, too, seemed to catch the mood of the moment, and the music became softer, sweeter, the strains of a Strauss waltz completely enveloping the two young lovers. All conversation ceased and we watched, fascinated. It was a happy and strangely moving scene as on and on the young couple waltzed, sweeping around and around the floor, hardly seeming to touch the parquetry, in a blaze of youthful exhiliration. They were completely oblivious of everyone else, totally concerned only with one another.

I looked at Amy. There were sudden tears in her eyes, bless her. I looked around us, and realized that everyone was oddly touched by this scene of young love, somehow so out of keeping with the champagne artificiality of the evening.

When the music finally ceased, Harry and Clare stood still. They remained facing one another, smiling shyly, not moving.

Someone clapped. Then another. Then everybody. Startled, the young couple looked around them in surprised embarrassment. Realizing their situation, Harry whispered to his partner and together they ran from the dance floor, through the onlookers, and out into one of the antechambers overlooking that open courtyard where Rodin's bronze *Balzac* gazes lecherously down on Henry Moore's gigantic recumbent mother-figure.

Almost as by way of relief, everybody laughed, indulgently.

Later in the evening, as I made my way through the throng, trying to find a waiter, to get fresh glasses of champagne for myself and Amy, I bumped into George Philanderer.

'I see that my Reader has made the acquaintance of your daughter, Judge,' I mentioned, by way of conversation, adopting the formal mode of address which a barrister always uses to a Judge in public, even if he is your cousin.

'Damn your Reader,' he replied savagely. 'I don't want my girl getting mixed up with some penniless barrister!'

'He's got quite a promising future,' I protested. 'I think he'll do very well at the Bar.'

'I won't have it, Dominic. I won't!' Philanderer retorted hotly. 'Just tell him to keep away from my daughter, or he'll have me to answer to.'

I was rather surprised at this vehemence, because Philanderer has always been a fairly easy-going chap, not the sort to play at the Barretts of Wimpole Street.

'I don't know what I can do about it, Judge,' I exclaimed. 'We can't stop young people falling in love, can we?'

'I won't have it, Dominic,' he repeated. 'I will forbid Clare ever to see him again.'

I looked at George . . . The same fair hair, now tinged with silver, the same grey eyes. I frowned.

'All right,' I replied, laying my hand calmingly on his arm, 'I'll speak to him,'

He seemed strangely relieved. 'Thank you, Dominic. I'd be much obliged to you, if you would.'

I did not see young Pomfret for the rest of the evening and had no opportunity to warn him that he had incurred the Judge's wrath. This was unfortunate, because—

After the ball Pomfret and Clare Philanderer went to that French restaurant in South Yarra that specializes in late-night *Crêpes Suzette*. Then Harry drove her home, on the back of his motorbike and she invited him in for a cup of coffee.

Closing the front door quietly behind them, they were tiptoeing across the wide, tiled entrance hall towards the kitchen when they became aware of His Honour himself, standing at the top of the staircase, in striped pyjamas and a dark-red satin dressing-gown.

'Hello Daddy,' Clare called, 'I had a lovely evening.'

Her father ignored her entirely. 'Young man,' he thundered, his resonant voice echoing around the entrance hall and the staircase, 'leave this house!'

Harry's jaw dropped and he stood in amazement.

'Leave this house!' Philanderer repeated, 'And never set foot in here again!'

'But Daddy—' Clare began, tearfully.

'Go to your room,' her father cut her short. 'I do not approve of your acquaintance with this person.'

'But—' she pleaded, sobbing.

'Go to your room at once. You are not to see him again. And you,' he turned towards Harry, 'Get out!'

Nothing more was said. Clare ran from the room. Without a word Harry Pomfret retraced his steps, leaving the front door wide open behind him.

For a long time Mr Justice Philanderer remained on the staircase, not moving, a worried unhappy expression on his face. Then he slowly descended the staircase, closed and locked the front door, and wandered to the library. There he poured himself a stiff brandy which he threw down in one gulp.

It is, as I had remarked to George Philanderer, impossible

In love with a judge's daughter

to stop young people falling in love, and Harry Pomfret and the Judge's daughter were undaunted by his displeasure. Indeed they seemed to become even more determined to see one another.

Clare Philanderer was a trainee social worker at the Peter MacCallum Hospital, only a stone's throw from Barristers' Chambers. Each lunch hour she and Harry would meet and walk to the nearby Flagstaff Gardens. There, beneath the giant elm trees and sitting on a park bench or on the grass, they would eat sandwiches Clare had prepared, and drink coffee from a thermos flask, in open defiance of the Judge's anger.

'Her father is not the sort of man to be crossed,' I warned Harry.

He looked at me and smiled, rather oddly. 'Neither am I,' he answered. 'I intend to marry Clare.'

'But your career,' I protested. 'If you make an enemy of a Supreme Court judge, it could do your career incalculable harm. The other judges will close ranks, you know. You'll find that you won't just have Philanderer dead set against you, but the whole Bench.'

Pomfret temporarily forgot the respect due to me, as his Master: His reply, a comment as to what the whole Bench of the Supreme Court might do, was very anatomical and quite scandalous. 'Sorry,' he added, quickly, 'but I intend to marry his daughter, whether he approves or not.'

That evening, as I practically sawed the serrations off a steak-knife in a despairing effort to cut through the *sole meunière* which Amy had prepared for my dinner, bless her, I confided to her the problems I was having with my Reader. She was singularly unsympathetic. The trouble with Amy is that she is a born romantic, and the plight of two young star-crossed lovers aroused in her all the tender compassion of a Barbara Cartland novel.

'The course of true love never runs smooth,' she sighed, then added, 'Anyway, George Philanderer is a stuffy spoil-sport.'

'He's always had a reputation to the contrary,' I protested mildly.

'He's a Capricorn,' she retorted quickly. 'I looked up his birth date in *Who's Who*, and he's a Capricorn. You know what they're like, Dominic. Oliver Cromwell was a Capricorn, and Hitler, and St Paul. That dreadful Captain Blight of the Bounty was too, and Mr Gladstone and Queen Victoria. Capricorn people are always stubborn and stuffy, and George Philanderer is behaving in exactly the way I would expect.'

I had by now given up the unequal struggle with the *sole meunière*, and Amy enquired anxiously, 'Aren't you hungry?'

'Not really,' I replied, diplomatically.

'You should finish it,' she assured me. 'I went to so much trouble cooking it for you. Besides, fish is brain food, and you need that, being a barrister. You can't expect to keep winning cases if you don't feed your brain, can you?'

I smiled feebly, picked up my knife and fork, and returned to the fray, under Amy's watchful eye, bless her.

'Gerard is coming for dinner on Saturday night,' she remarked. 'He's bringing his new girl-friend. I do hope she's nice. And Catholic. Did you know that awful girl he was with at the Arts Ball was a *Methodist*? I can't understand Gerard, after all the money we spent on his education. I'm sure the Jesuits must have warned him not to fall in love with a Methodist.'

'I imagine the good Fathers had so much trouble teaching him the binomial theorem,' I sighed, 'that there was not sufficient time left to warn him against Methodists.'

'I'm not saying there's anything wrong with Methodists, Dominic. Some of my best friends on the Cerebro-Spinal-Spastic Committee are Methodists. But they are different aren't they? I mean . . . Anyway, I wouldn't like my son to marry one.'

I didn't reply. I couldn't. Not with a mouthful of Amy's *sole meunière*.

'I thought it would be a good idea if you asked your young Mr Pomfret to dinner at the same time,' she continued.

'Mm . . . mm . . . mm,' I agreed.

'And I'll ask some nice girl, to make up the numbers,' she concluded, triumphantly.

'Mm . . . mm . . . mm.' If my jaws had not been trapped around a piece of brain food, I would have asked Who?

'Well, that's all settled. I'll just go and ring Gerard to see if he's free on Saturday night.'

I swallowed, painfully. 'I thought you said he was already coming for dinner on Saturday night?'

'Well, so he is,' she called back as she left the room, 'but he won't come if I don't invite him, will he?'

I let the matter drop. If you live with a woman long enough, in the end you learn not to ask too many sensible questions, bless her.

DINNER AT EIGHT, CHEZ AMY

'My wife thought you might like to come to dinner on Saturday night,' I mentioned to Harry Pomfret the next morning.

He smiled, 'Thank you.'

'Seven-thirty for eight o'clock: Will that be convenient?'

'Yes.' He paused, then shyly asked, 'What should I wear?' Sometimes the gaucherie of the younger generation astonishes me.

'You are invited for dinner,' I answered. 'I assume you have a dinner suit? Or,' I enquired, somewhat maliciously, 'do you hire one?'

He blushed, and didn't reply.

When I came out of Court that morning, my clerk had a message for me: 'Mr Justice Philanderer's Associate said His Honour would like to see you this afternoon, after Court, if it's convenient.'

I considered. What cousin George wanted to say to me, and what I might want to say to him would perhaps take some time. 'You'd better cancel my appointment for a conference this afternoon, Arthur,' I said. 'Tell the solicitor I'll confer with his client on Friday at 5.30 instead.'

Arthur hesitated. 'They're a very reliable firm of solicitors—always pay on the knocker. We don't want to offend them, do we?'

'Give the solicitor my abject apologies—terribly sorry—wouldn't for the world—unavoidable—have to see a Supreme Court judge.'

'You don't get paid for talking to a Supreme Court judge,' Arthur grumbled. 'I don't know why he couldn't talk to you later in the evening, at his club.'

'Now, Arthur, don't be difficult. Just cancel my conference and make a new appointment.'

'It's not good for business,' he muttered as he wandered off, shaking his head. Arthur always has my interests at heart. And why not? We feed off the same carcass.

'Sorry I'm late, Judge,' I apologized breathlessly, 'but your brother Merryweather didn't adjourn his Court at the usual hour.'

Philanderer spread his hands, deprecatingly, and smiled. 'Do you take lemon or milk with your tea?'

'Lemon, please.'

Philanderer glanced in the direction of his tipstaff, presiding over the sterling silver tea-service at an occasional table before the tall windows of His Honour's Chambers. 'So glad you could spare the time to drop in, Dominic. I hope you didn't have to cancel a conference?'

'Nothing of consequence, Judge,' I replied, wishing his tipstaff would hurry up and pour the tea, and go.

'Is Amy well?'

'Yes. Still busy with all her charity committees, as usual.'

We smiled politely at one another. The tipstaff handed me a cup of tea and a serviette, and left, closing the door quietly behind him.

'Would you care for a cake, or a biscuit?' Philanderer asked, indicating the silver salver at my elbow.

I placed my cup of tea to one side, and, now that the tipstaff was gone, dropped the formalities. 'What did you want to see me about, George?'

Philanderer frowned slightly, and seemed to choose his words with care.

'It's your pupil, Dominic. He's still seeing my daughter.'

'I understand he wants to marry her.'

The Judge stood up and walked to the window, his back towards me. 'I won't allow it,' he said, quietly but determinedly. Then turning around, he went on, 'Look, Dominic, you and I have been through the mill. We both know what a life it is for a woman being married to a barrister. He's never home. Every night, every weekend he's working. He's always working. He's always got a case to prepare, some world-shattering case that he's got to win. His wife and his children play second fiddle to his career.'

'Your wife coped with all that, George. Mine did too. Why couldn't your daughter?'

Philanderer came back and sat down. For a minute he was silent, and then at length he replied, 'I only have one child, Dominic, and I want her to get the best out of life. I'm not short of money. My parents left me very comfortably off, and I also invested the earnings I made at the Bar wisely. I'm sure to receive a knighthood at the New Year's Honours List: I'm the next judge on the ladder.'

I nodded agreement.

'Clare has everything going for her,' he continued, 'an assured social position, enough money to live up to it. When it comes to husbands, she can pick and choose. And I don't intend her to choose someone on the bottom rung of a very tough profession.'

I stirred my tea, considering. 'George,' I asked gently, 'is that the only reason you are so dead-set against my Reader marrying your daughter?'

'What do you mean?' he suddenly blustered.

'Young Pomfret tells me his father is a judge,' I went on, very calmly, 'but he doesn't know which one.'

Philanderer gazed steadily at me, poker-faced. Not a muscle moved, not a nerve twitched.

'He looks very like you, when you were young, George,' I continued.

The Judge snorted, 'What nonsense! What a ridiculous idea! I've never heard such a piece of claptrap! As if I would—'

'Come off it, George,' I interrupted him. 'I know you're a Supreme Court judge and all that. But we're alone. There's nobody else here, so don't play the high and mighty with me.'

'I don't know what could have put such an idea into your head,' he half-shouted, angrily.

'Young Pomfret is precisely twenty-four years of age,' I retorted. 'And twenty-four years ago you weren't so goody-goody.'

He went to speak, but I motioned to him to be silent. 'Do you remember that time we went out to the Royal Show? Those two girls with the show-bags?'

'That's got nothing to do with this matter,' he remonstrated.

'And the time we got drunk together at the Frankston Pier Hotel? Those other two girls? Mine was called Beatrice, if I remember correctly,' I reminisced. 'What was your one's name?'

'. . . Marguerite,' he ground out.

'I wondered at the time what book they read those names in,'

I continued reflectingly. 'And the Easter weekend we spent at the Shamrock Hotel at Bendigo, with the two girls from the Arts Faculty?'

'I don't understand why you're dragging up all these gone and forgotten youthful indiscretions.'

'Because,' now *I* raised my voice, 'because Harry Pomfret was conceived at the Pig and Whistle Hotel in the Blue Mountains on the Queen's Birthday weekend in 1956!'

We were both silent.

'Now what I want to know, George Philanderer,' I said, 'and I want a truthful answer, and it won't go beyond these four walls, but are you Harry Pomfret's father?'

Philanderer at first did not reply. When he did, it was in a husky tone, 'No, I am not.'

'You're quite sure?' I insisted.

'I give you my word.'

'Well,' I said, standing, 'that's good enough for me.'

'I only want what's best for my daughter, Dominic,' the Judge shook his head.

'Well, there's not much that I can do, but I'll do what I can.'

'I thought that perhaps you might advise him to apply for a position as a Magistrate or a Crown Prosecutor in Hong Kong? They're always advertising for Australian barristers to go there.'

'I doubt whether he's experienced enough for that, George.'

'I understand there are lots of good openings for a young barrister in the Northern Territory.'

'I don't know, I don't know,' I replied glumly. 'As my pupil I can regulate his professional life, but his private life is something over which I have very little control. Couldn't you send Clare away for a while?'

'I've suggested it, but she refuses.'

'I'll talk to him again, George,' I promised, and prepared to leave.

As I reached the door, Philanderer said quickly, 'I hope you won't repeat to anybody that you thought I was your Reader's father, Dominic. I mean, it would be very embarrassing for me. It might even scotch my chances of a knighthood. And my wife . . .'

'You've told me you're not his father and I accept your word for that. There's no way I'm likely to go around spreading malicious slanders about you.'

And on that, I left.

I decided that the best time to tackle young Pomfret on the subject would be on the Saturday night. Amy's idea of inviting him to dinner could not have come at a more opportune moment. I could leave Gerard to talk to the girls while I showed Pomfret my library, and that would give me the opportunity to broach the subject. Yes, Saturday night would be just the right occasion . . .

When Saturday night came, Gerard and his new girl-friend arrived early. This girl was Catholic, all right, but that was the only thing she had going for her. I never met such a dunce in my life. Her name was Amelia Mutt, and she had a carefully cultivated lisp. All she did all night long was giggle and simper, 'Oh, Geward . . . ' I don't think I heard her utter one complete sentence the whole evening.

Young Pomfret rang the front door bell at precisely 7.30. He had in fact arrived early and had to walk twice around the block to fill in the time.

Gerard busied himself handing around the sherry while we waited for the girl Amy had invited 'to make up the numbers.' 7.40 and she still was not there . . . 7.45 . . . 7.50 . . . At three minutes to eight the doorbell rang, and Amy bustled to the entrance hall.

'So glad you could come,' she trilled. 'I was becoming quite anxious. Come along in, dear, and meet everybody.'

And there in the doorway stood George Philanderer's daughter, Clare!

I put my hands to my head in despair, and recalled, with understanding and approval, Mr Justice Buller's decision in 1782 that a man may lawfully beat his wife with a stick, provided that the stick is no thicker than his thumb.

At eight o'clock exact, we sat down to dinner. Half-way through the soup Amy, bless her, remarked to Clare, 'I hear your father is opposed to your friendship.' I coughed and hurriedly changed the subject.

Half-way through the entree, Amy tried again, 'It must be very difficult for you and Harry, having to see one another in secret.' I immediately plunged into a frenzied and irrelevant speech about how the murderer Haig confessed to sucking the blood of his victims through a lemonade straw.

Half-way through the fish course, Amy observed, 'If you give him time, dear, I'm sure your father will come around to your way of thinking.' The dinner guests were post-haste subjected to a long and exhausting diatribe on my views of what was wrong with Collingwood Football Club, a speech so vehemently and desperately delivered, that they all sat there in stunned silence.

Half-way through the meat course, Amy, smiling encouragingly at Clare and Harry, asked, 'When do you two plan to get married?' Then, turning quickly to me, she added, 'And I'd be obliged if you didn't interrupt this time, Dominic.'

The conversation that ensued lasted through the meat course, the dessert, the cheese and greens, the coffee and after-dinner mints. It was a marathon, Amy offering as much good advice to these latter-day Romeo and Juliet as would have filled the agony columns of *The Women's Weekly* for a year or more, punctuated by irrelevant squeals of 'Oh Geward . . . Oh Geward . . . ' from Amelia Mutt.

Clare Philanderer was a most attractive girl, with a flawless complexion, and the same searching grey eyes as Harry. Her fair wavy hair was silken and hung loosely to her shoulders with a carefully contrived air of nonchalance. She wore no jewellery. Her pale blue evening gown was cut low, revealing a smooth, lightly tanned throat and shoulders. She laughed readily, chattered brightly, was obviously intelligent and it was little wonder that Harry Pomfret was besotted of her.

For his part, he was very much her masculine replica—the jaw more firm, the eye more keen, the hair short, the body more taut, the shoulders more square, but the likeness was uncanny. Even the way they laughed was similar. If I had not had George Philanderer's assurance that they were unrelated, I would have started worrying all over again. People talk about the attraction of opposites, but in the case of Harry and Clare, the attraction was positively narcissistic.

I did not add much to the general conversation. After my interview with Clare's father, the whole scene was decidedly embarrassing. But towards the end of the evening, over coffee and liqueurs, Clare looked directly at me, and asked challengingly, 'And what do *you* think we should do, Uncle?'

I gazed thoughtfully at her and did not immediately reply. Finally I said simply, 'I think that Harry should not offend your father.'

The shaft went home. If I had replied, 'I do not think *you* should offend your father,' no doubt she would have disregarded my advice. But I had disturbed her.

'Why?' she asked, uncertainly.

I contented myself with repeating, without elaboration, 'I think Harry should not offend your father.'

There was a sudden lull in the conversation. Perhaps it was because, until then, I had had very little to contribute to the general discussion, perhaps it was the studied definiteness of my response, but the atmosphere at the table had now become tense, uneasy.

'What do you think we should do?' Clare asked.

Again I paused before replying. 'Your father probably thinks that this is some passing infatuation on your part, that has got out of hand. Why don't you go away for a while, to think things over?'

Gerard and Harry Pomfret immediately started to protest, but were swiftly put down. 'I am your father,' I said to Gerard, 'and your Master,' I said to Pomfret, 'and I won't be interrupted by either of you. Now be quiet when I speak, or else go and play snooker in the billiard room.'

They lapsed into obedient silence, albeit very grudgingly, while Amelia giggled, 'Oh, Geward . . .'

'You can transfer your training as a social worker to another hospital, in Sydney, or Adelaide,' I continued. 'If at the end of six months you still feel the same about my pupil, I'm sure your father would be more easily reconciled to the fact.'

'And if I don't?'

'I think that Harry should not offend your father,' I repeated.

'You are probably right,' she said quietly, at last. 'What do you say, Harry?'

'I say he's wrong!' he exclaimed, then glancing at me, he added, 'With all due respect.'

'Oh Geward . . . ' Amelia cooed.

'I don't think so,' Clare replied. 'Just think of your career. How successful would a young barrister be, if his father-in-law was a Judge who refused to speak to him? I've lived in a lawyer's house all my life, and if there's one thing I've learnt, it's that they all stick together.'

'That doesn't matter, as long as I win my cases,' he replied.

'Oh Geward . . . '

'You wouldn't win any,' Clare declared. 'The other judges would see to that. And the solicitors wouldn't send you any briefs, anyway. I think it's true that you should not offend my father. I think I should go away for a while, and let things settle down.'

'Oh Geward . . . '

Later that night, in bed, Amy said reproachfully, 'You really are perfectly horrible, Dominic, telling Clare to go and live in Sydney or Adelaide. She is obviously head over heels in love with Harry Pomfret, and he is with her, too.'

'What do you think of Gerard's new girl-friend?' I asked, to change the subject.

'Perfectly charming,' Amy gushed. 'Delightful.'

'You don't think she's a bit stupid?'

'Not at all. She's just the girl I would have chosen for him myself.'

'I suppose that's right,' I replied, and turned over and went to sleep.

I deemed it wise to telephone cousin George the next day, to inform him that I thought I had succeeded in persuading Clare to go away for a while. It also seemed appropriate to warn him, before somebody else did so, that Amy, bless her, had invited both Harry and Clare to our place for dinner.

But I was too late. He already knew.

'After our conversation the other day, I consider that a very unfriendly gesture on your part, Dominic,' he said tersely, and he had hung up before I had time to tell him the good news.

Several days later I had the ill chance to be briefed to appear in an action for breach of contract before Mr Justice Philanderer. My instructing solicitor and my unfortunate client were amazed at the rapidity with which I lost their case.

'The Judge didn't seem to like you much,' my client naively complained.

My instructing solicitor said nothing, but looked grim, no doubt worrying how he was going to recover his costs.

I must say that, from the day Pomfret had first set foot in my Chambers, I seemed to have been dogged by bad luck. I was more than a little worried. Once a barrister starts on a run of losing cases, his practice can dwindle dramatically overnight. There is always a plethora of young, ambitious, unemployed barristers waiting in the wings, itching to push us established Counsel off stage. I would have to look to my laurels, if Amy and I were not to spend our old age dependent on the kindnesses of the St. Vincent de Paul Society.

A COUPLE OF SHOP-FRONT JUDGES

Each year, at the beginning of the legal term, it is customary for judges, barristers, solicitors and law clerks to go to pray in the Melbourne cathedrals. This ritual is always accompanied by pomp and ceremony, with processions of judges and barristers in robes, all sweltering it out in the hot February sun. Of course the *hoi polloi* love it. It gives them an opportunity to gaze wide-eyed and open-mouthed as the judges parade in public in all their forensic finery, scarlet robes with blue trimmings, black sashes, full-bottomed wigs, billowing white lace cuffs at the wrist, billowing white lace cravats, black knee breeches, black silk stockings, silver buckles on their shoes. Then, having besought and perhaps obtained divine guidance, Their Honours depart from the cathedrals and go back to their courts, where they can forget about God for the next twelve months.

They do reappear however, from time to time during the year. On formal State occasions, bewigged and berobed, they form a solid, sweeping scarlet phalanx, all wearing their most wise and most solemn Easter Island faces, just to remind the politicians that none of *them,* be he backbencher or Cabinet Minister, is above the law.

But on one occasion this symbolic display of the might and power of the Courts, went off like a damp squib. It was December, shortly before Christmas, and, in celebration of a Royal visit, the Judiciary were to attend a civic reception in the Town Hall. Ceremonially garbed, they left in carloads from the Law Courts, and the limousines in due course pulled up outside the portico of the Town Hall. The streets were crowded. It was already school holidays and the Mums were in town with their children, doing their last-minute Christmas shopping.

As the judges alighted from their cars, there was a sudden scream of excitement. Every kid within viewing distance went mad with delight, waving, cheering themselves hoarse. They had never seen so many Santa Claus clones all together before. Very sheepishly Their Honours betook themselves in their scarlet robes and full-bottomed wigs into the safety of the Town Hall before the kids had time to capture them, and tell them what they wanted for Christmas.

Then, at the conclusion of this civic reception, and after the departure of Her Majesty and entourage, the judges at length reappeared under the portico, the Lord Mayor in his heavily gold-braided robes, white lace jabot and gold chain of office, presiding at the ritual of their official farewell. And once again, at the sight of all the Father Christmases, the kids in the crowd behind the barricades let out a sudden frenzied scream of delight, of such piercing intensity that the mounted police had trouble restraining their horses and simultaneously holding their flag-bedecked lances steady at attention.

Amid the deafening squeals of the tiny tots and as speedily as decorum permitted, the judges re-entered their waiting limousines and their procession began, back to the Law Courts. On the way their cars travelled via Lonsdale Street, now almost deserted, because everyone had hurried to the streets around the Town Hall, in the hope of a chance to see the Queen. Harry Pomfret happened to be one of the few people in Lonsdale Street at the time the Judges' procession passed. He was standing on the very edge of the footpath outside the Myer Emporium, waiting to cross the road, when a most extraordinary thing occurred.

In one of the cars there were three judges: Mr Justice Philanderer was sitting in the front, next to the driver; Mr Justice Dott and Mr Justice Dashe were in the back seat. As they approached the place where Harry was standing, this car suddenly and without any warning changed course and veered erratically to the edge of the road, straight at Harry. Only by leaping desperately sideways did he avoid being run over.

The Judges' car, now completely out of control, mounted the footpath and continued on, straight through one of the Myer's display windows, with a shattering explosion of flying glass, the window-dressers' dummies hurtling in all directions. The car then smashed its way into one of the supporting pillars of the window with such devastating effect that a cross-beam above was dislodged and fell, completely crushing the rear section of the car. By a miracle, the driver and George Philanderer escaped unhurt, but Mr Justice Dott and Mr Justice Dashe in the back seat (may God have mercy on their souls!) were squashed quite flat, poached-egg shape, scarlet blobs with ermine edging, sunnyside up.

When the police arrived, the driver, no doubt desperately searching for some excuse for his gross carelessness, came up with the cock-and-bull story that, just before the accident, one of the Judges had unexpectedly seized the steering wheel and caused the car to change direction, over towards where Harry was standing. Of course nobody believed such arrant nonsense. Much later that day, the driver, no doubt having given the matter some serious thought, and also probably having received some sound advice, had the good sense to change his story and take all the blame, like a man.

They charged him with careless driving, of course—indeed how could they do otherwise, with two Judges dead?—but he wasn't convicted. I must say that his acquittal was due in no small measure to the good offices of George Philanderer who readily volunteered to appear as a witness on his behalf. At the hearing, His Honour's evidence was so generous and so fulsome in praise of the defendant, saying how careful a driver he always was, and how the car had suddenly got out of control despite all the defendant's desperate efforts to steer it, that there was no possibility of a conviction. The car itself was such a mess, a total write-off, that it was impossible for the forensic science experts even to guess at the cause of the vehicle's erratic behaviour.

In my opinion this was a very sporting gesture on the part of Mr Justice Philanderer, seeing that the carelessness of the driver could easily have killed him too. Like the other two unfortunate Judges.

'Who do you think they will—' Pomfret began.

'*Whom . . .*' I sighed, '*Whom . . .*'

A Santa Claus clone

THE SMILE OF THE CROCODILE

I received the following note, hand-delivered by Mr Justice Philanderer's Associate:

Dear Dominic,

Sorry I was so abrupt on the phone. Please accept my apologies for the misunderstanding. Clare informs me that you advised her to go away for a while and she intends to do so. She has arranged a transfer of her training to Prince of Wales Hospital in Sydney for six months. My best wishes to Amy.

Gratefully,
George.

His Honour might have been well satisfied with this turn of events, but not so my pupil. I had never seen such a sulky young brute. If looks could kill, I would have dropped dead in my tracks.

'If I am found one night in some dark alley, with a knife in my back,' I warned Amy, 'tell the Police that Harry Pomfret did it.'

'Don't talk nonsense, Dominic,' she declared. 'Don't you like the nasi goreng?'

'Delicious,' I lied, smacking my lips. 'Superb!'

'You don't look as though you like it. Perhaps all this worry over Clare Philanderer has spoilt your appetite.'

'Yes, that must be it,' I replied, thankful for any excuse and pushing my plate to one side. 'The worry has turned me off my food.'

'I'll cook you something extra-appetizing for tomorrow night,' she promised.

I groaned inwardly. 'No need to go to a lot of trouble,' I suggested soothingly. 'Sausages and mash would be fine.'

But she was not listening, bless her. 'Your star signs are not propitious at the moment,' she went on. 'The Sun is in Aries and the Moon is in Leo. You must avoid arguments and confrontations, it says in the paper.'

'How do I avoid arguments and confrontations, if I've got to defend people in Court every day?'

'There you go!' Amy exclaimed triumphantly. 'You're arguing already.'

'I'm not arguing.'

'You are, Dominic, you're always arguing.'

'I'm not.'

'Of course you are.'

'I am not.'

'Yes, you are, dear. I ought to know, after twenty-five years of marriage.'

'Really, Amy, you make me sound like a bear.'

'But you are a bear, Dominic, a very argumentative bear, and if I was poor Harry Pomfret I would certainly stick a knife in your back the first opportunity I got.'

The next morning, Pomfret was as surly as ever. I watched him thoughtfully as, with no good grace, he attempted to draft a difficult Statement of Claim.

'My wife says that if she were you, she would stick a knife in my back,' I remarked.

Pomfret looked up from his work, in some slight amazement, then suddenly burst into laughter. 'You may thank her for the suggestion,' he replied. 'I hadn't thought of it, but it's a wonderful idea.'

After that, the ice was broken and I was spared the daily sight of a thwarted young lover, brooding over his hurt pride.

Pomfret was by now beginning to build up quite a respectable practice for one so recently called to the Bar. But the methods by which he was doing so were very questionable in my opinion.

Not content with an assortment of religious observances on Sunday mornings, he devoted the rest of the Sabbath to political activities. Sunday lunch he spent eating thick sandwiches and drinking black tea out of chipped mugs with the Socialist left. He then motor-biked to a weekly meeting of the Labour Party Right-wing. Then off to a barbecue with the Young Liberals.

He always carried appropriate clothing in a bag on the back of his motor cycle and changed en route. For the Socialist left he wore a collar and conservative tie, formal black jacket and striped pants. For the Right-wing Labour group he wore an open-neck white shirt, sports coat and slacks. For the Little Liberals, he wore a Yakka shirt and jeans. They loved it. The Socialist Left, who revel in snobbery, thought he added quite a touch of class to their reunions. The Young Liberals, who revel in inverted snobbery, thought he demonstrated the fact that they were getting their message through to the working man.

There were always plenty of solicitor hangers-on at these political orgies, secretly hoping that one day they would win nomination for a seat in Parliament. There was no way they could fail to notice Harry, and they all sent him briefs. One day he would appear in Court for some financial member of the Waterside Workers Federation, on a charge of indecently exposing himself to a group of basketball players at a Western Suburbs Girls School. The next day he would appear for the Chairman of the Board of a multinational corporation, arrested for indecently exposing himself to a group of croquet players at a Presbyterian Ladies' College.

If he had time, in between his Sunday political junketing, Harry would drop in to a barrel party at the Carlton Football Club or the Melbourne Football Club, sing a few drunken songs, shake hands with every solicitor there present, and slap them on the back, then jump on his motor-bike and off to his next rendezvous.

Sunday was his busiest working day in the week. And the briefs flowed in. They were only to appear in Magistrates' Courts, piddling matters, but all good experience.

But the quest for his father remained his one burning obsession.

'If only I knew who he was,' he lamented.

'Well, we drew a blank with Melchior, Applebaum and Kneebone,' I said, crossing myself, out of respect, 'and Clare's father has assured me that *he* is not your father.'

Pomfret looked at me in sudden surprise. 'I'd forgotten he was on your list.'

'He was, but is no longer. He has given me his solemn assurance.'

'Who is left then?'

I ticked them off my fingers: 'Sir Anthony Opscotch . . . and Mr Justice Cumquat. For your sake, I hope it's not Cumquat.'
'Is he really as terrible as everybody says?'
'Like the curate's egg, he is good in parts. But he still stinks. I suggest we leave him until last, and if the other judge is ruled out, you would be well advised to give up. Better no father than Cumquat.'
'What makes him so awful?'
'Shortness of stature. He's only 5 feet nothing. When he was at school the other kids teased him and bullied him because he was smaller than they were. When he was at University, none of the girls wanted to dance with him at parties, because he was too short. When he came to the Bar, he used to tack a raise on to the heels of his shoes to make himself look taller. Can you imagine what that does to a person's ego?'
'It would be very mortifying, I suppose.'
'Now that he's on the Bench, clothed in a little bit of authority, he's taking his revenge on the world. Let's hope, Harry Pomfret, that you weren't sired by Mr Justice Cumquat.'
'And the other one?'
'Opscotch is all right. Has a wife and eleven children—all girls, and all giggly. They drive him mad. He goes fishing every weekend to get away from them. Owns a three-legged dog that follows him everywhere. He even takes it into Court. It sits on a chair beside him but you can't see it because of the height of the bench. One day it barked in the middle of a trial. I can assure you, if you happen to be Sir Anthony's son, he will welcome you with outstretched arms. Be a relief after all those giggling girls.'
'Well, I hope Mr Justice Opscotch is the one who is my father.'
'Yes, he'd be tickled pink. But,' I cautioned, 'first catch your rabbit.'
'How?'
'I think it's high time, young Pomfret, that you took a trip to the Pig and Whistle, to see if they still have the house guest register for 1956. They often do keep them for years and years in these old country hotels.'
'What good will that do?'
'Have you never stayed at a country hotel? They ask everyone to sign the register. That means that your father's handwriting

should be there for you to inspect. Admittedly he almost certainly would have used a false name—Mr and Mrs John Smith, or Mr and Mrs William Brown—but he probably wouldn't take the precaution of changing his handwriting.'

'And then?'

'I'll get photostat copies of Chambers Orders signed by both judges, Opscotch and Cumquat, and you can compare the handwriting. How about that?'

Harry gazed at me, with a certain respect, as I telephoned a few solicitors I knew, to enquire if they had an Order made in Chambers signed by either of the two judges. Within an hour we had the photostats. I held them up for my Reader to see.

'One of those signatures, my boy,' I declaimed, 'is that of your Daddy!'

But the next day Pomfret was glum again. Clare had that morning departed for Sydney. She came to see me before she left.

I was in the Criminal Court, in the middle of my closing address, orating away, inviting the jury to just look at my respectable innocent client there in the dock, just look at him, you couldn't possibly believe, not for one moment, that such a fine, upstanding, respectable, innocent man would be guilty of fraud, embezzlement, forgery, false pretences, assault occasioning grievous bodily harm, drug trafficking, bigamy, rape, manslaughter, burglary, unlawful possession of firearms, and parking his car in a No Standing zone . . . The Accused was a Member of Parliament, so the trial had attracted some public attention and the Court was crowded. As I dramatically waved my arms around in the air, in a desperate effort to divert the jury's attention from some trifling weaknesses in my respectable, innocent client's story, I noticed among all the other façes in the public gallery, the face of Harry Pomfret. I vaguely wondered what the devil he was doing up there, when he could have been sitting down behind me, in the well of the Court.

When the Court was adjourned, I glanced up again at the public gallery and realised, with a start, that it was not Harry I had seen, but Clare. As I was leaving the Court she came up, slipped her hand under the voluminous sleeves of my gown, and took my arm.

'I'll walk you back to Chambers,' she said.

He was too short

I patted her hand: 'There's a compliment for an old dog. You'll make my pupil jealous,' I warned her.

She laughed. 'Did you know I was going to Sydney for six months?'

'Your father told me, but I might have guessed, with Harry raging around as if the end of the world was about to happen.'

She laughed again. Indeed she laughed very prettily, that girl. 'You do think I'm doing the right thing, don't you?' she asked, somewhat anxiously.

I glanced at her. The same fair wavy hair, the same grey eyes, the same well-formed features . . . It still worried me, even though I knew she and Harry were not related. I was thankful George Philanderer had assured me of that.

'I'm certain you should,' I replied. 'Better to let things simmer down for a while. I don't want Harry starting off his professional career on the wrong foot, with a Supreme Court judge on his back.'

She seemed much reassured. 'I wasn't certain . . .'

Harry was in Chambers when we arrived there, his desk piled high with opened volumes of law reports.

'Hello, Master,' he murmured, without lifting his head from his work.

'Hello, Slave,' I replied. 'Have you met my latest girl-friend?'

He looked up and grinned. 'I'll take her off your hands, if you don't mind.' He pushed his work to one side and stood up.

As they were leaving, Clare paused and came back to my desk. 'I hope you win your case,' she whispered, and gave me a peck on the cheek. Then off they went, treading on air.

Her good wishes availed me nothing. My fine, upstanding, respectable, innocent client got 54 years hard labour, and his licence to drive a motor car was cancelled for 3 months.

'I say, Dominic,' Macquarie Q.C. said, waving in the air a fish fork in one hand and a glass of Riesling in the other, 'what gives with your Reader?'

I raised my eyebrows in surprise: 'What do you mean?'

Macquarie sniffed at his Riesling and sipped. Macquarie is incapable of drinking a glass of wine without sniffing at it first. Like a dog with offal. 'Nice bouquet . . . I would say 1975 . . . Hunter Valley . . . Well, has he put a jinx on the Supreme court Bench?'

'What do you mean?' I repeated.

'Surely it can't have escaped your attention that the judges are falling off the twig like flies.'

'I had heard,' I smiled, 'but I hadn't noticed.'

'Well, dash it all, every time one of them goes off, your pupil Pomfret is on the spot.'

The rest of the table looked up from their meal with interest.

'It was his golf ball that killed Kneebone,' Macquarie went on, aware that he had a captive audience, 'and he was sitting right next to Melchior here in the Common Room when *he* choked to death.' Everyone had by now stopped eating. 'And Applebaum – no sooner had your Reader climbed that ladder and spoken to him, than Applebaum jumped. And now Dashe and Dott – Pomfret was right there in Lonsdale Street when they got theirs.'

'A mere coincidence,' I remarked.

'Perhaps he has the evil eye,' Hammersmith laughed.

'It's deuced odd,' Macquarie went on, 'If I were a Supreme Court judge, I'd steer clear of your pupil. If we keep losing judges at this rate, there'll be none left.'

'I hear the Attorney-General is at his wit's end, trying to puzzle out whom to appoint in their places,' Parsifal added.

'A rash of elevations of the Bench will leave the Senior Bar very thin,' Macquarie continued, sniffed again at his Riesling, and sipped.

But there was one Judge, anyway, who was apparently not of the opinion that Pomfret had a hoodoo on the Bench. Several days after Clare had left for Sydney, a very surprising thing happened.

'Mr Justice Philanderer's Associate says His Honour sends his compliments, and would it be convenient for you to have lunch with him at his Club on Thursday?' Arthur remarked.

'Will I have time?'

'I think so,' Arthur counted on his fingers. 'That Appeal of yours will dribble over into Thursday morning, so they say, which will leave you with the rest of the day free.'

'All right. Accept.'

'Oh, and he also extended the invitation to your pupil.'

'Pomfret?'

'Yes,' Arthur nodded, 'though I can't for the life of me imagine why a Supreme Court judge would want to invite anybody's pupil to lunch. Most odd. They could hardly have anything in common.'

'They're probably both interested in the same girl,' I remarked, playfully.

Arthur looked properly shocked.

George Philanderer's Club, I thought with some envy, was much grander than my own Celtic Club. From the minute we walked through the entrance doors, their half-glass panels embossed with sand-blasted floral motifs of the Victorian Age, we entered a quiet, subdued, other world. The carpets were costly, but comfortably worn. The lounge chairs, upholstered in the finest hide, were also comfortably worn. The rich velvet drapes on either side of the tall windows must have been at least forty years of age, and were fastened back by coils of dull gilt rope. The crisp sparkle of crystal of the wide-spreading chandeliers was duplicated in large mirrors encased in carved walnut frames. The century-old waxed and hand-polished Victorian furniture and the silver warming-dishes on the marble-topped credenzas shone with the deep rich glow of reflected light.

The table, to which the shirt-sleeved striped-waistcoated waiter showed us, was dressed with a heavily starched white table-cloth hanging almost to the floor. In the centre of this table stood an elegant *épergne*, its fluted vases filled with fresh flowers, its fruit bowl offering us an assortment of apples, pears, peaches, bananas, and grapes. The cutlery was simple, but sterling. Yes, definitely a step above the Celtic Club . . .

I glanced at Harry. He was obviously impressed and I wondered how long it would be before he contrived to get himself nominated as a member of this prestige preserve.

'Glad you could come,' Philanderer said, as a waiter handed us the hand-written menu. 'I would recommend the fish. The cook has a way with it.' At Philanderer's Club there is no chef—only a cook. The menu is never typed or printed, always hand-written. They serve pudding, not dessert. The labels on expensive wine bottles are always hidden by a serviette. Tea and coffee are never served at the table, but after, in the club room.

During the meal, Clare's name was not mentioned once. Indeed, it was carefully avoided. His Honour was the perfect host and went out of his way to make Harry and me feel at ease.

He enquired after Amy's health, how Gerard was getting on with his medical practice in South Yarra, whether it was our Parish priest who had given character evidence in a case before him the other day. Then he wanted to know what sorts of briefs Pomfret was getting, whether he was busy, what were his professional ambitions.

'I intend to be a Supreme Court judge,' Harry replied promptly.

For a moment I was afraid Philanderer might bridle at such brashness on the part of a mere boy, still with only half a foot on the bottom rung of the legal ladder, but he seemed mightily amused. 'Rome wasn't built in a day,' he remarked.

'That was because they didn't know they were building Rome,' Harry came in quickly. 'If they had, they might have got a move on.'

His Honour laughed indulgently, and slid back the lid of the sterling silver butter-cooler. I was again eaten with envy: At the Celtic Club we would hardly know what to do with a butter-cooler. Somebody there would probably drink out of it . . .

At an adjoining table I could overhear two very quietly dressed men nonchalantly devising a take-over scheme for B.H.P. At a table on the other side three very quietly dressed men were listening as a fourth just as nonchalantly canvassed their support for his plan to send Conzinc Rio Tinto to the wall.

'To succeed at the Bar,' Philanderer was counselling Harry, 'you must build up a stable of different firms of solicitors to send you work, so that you are constantly in Court.'

'I hardly think my pupil is unaware of that ploy,' I remarked, and gave a laconic description of his religious and political Sunday activities.

If I expected His Honour to be horrified by such duplicity, I was disappointed. He was, on the contrary, frankly delighted. 'Good boy, good boy,' he exclaimed, encouragingly. 'You should join the Junior Chamber of Commerce, too. I'll arrange for your nomination, if you wish.'

I had known George Philanderer for a long time, and it occurred to me that, for some reason, he was going out of his way to charm Harry Pomfret. George never was one to flatter anybody, but he was giving the definite impression that in his eyes, Pomfret could do no wrong.

'When you have finished Reading law,' he said, as we sat later in the club room, drinking coffee and smoking cigars which had, at a glance from His Honour, suddenly materialized on a silver tray held by a striped-waistcoated waiter, 'when you have finished your Reading, you will have to take Chambers of your own.' He paused, puffed at his cigar, 'I have a spare set of the All England Law Reports I don't use much, and Halsbury's Laws, and the Australian Legal Digest. They might come in handy for you.'

Now I understood! Philanderer was making a take-over bid, in the casual fashion of his Club. At the Celtic, we'd call it a bribe. I waited for the crunch which would come before we left, I felt sure.

'A young barrister like you needs all the help he can get,' George went on, patronizingly. 'I can probably give you a hand along the way. I know a few solicitors who are always looking for a promising young colt to brief.' He smiled amiably. 'I have no doubt you'll do well at the Bar, my boy, if you play your cards right.'

Harry stammered his thanks, obviously overwhelmed by the great man's kindness.

'And how do you intend to spend the long vacation? Christmas is almost upon us,' His Honour asked, in a disinterested fashion, idly turning the gold signet ring on one of his fingers, its face catching and reflecting the light, and winking, as it revolved.

I hurried to answer that one. 'Pomfret has not finished his Reading and will be required to remain in Chambers.' I imagined a fleeting shadow of relief passed across Philanderer's face, and could not prevent myself from adding, mischievously, 'Of course, he can take off the days between Christmas and the New Year. He wants to go to the Blue Mountains, to inspect the house-guest register of the Pig and Whistle Hotel.' Turning to Harry, I said, 'I suppose you'll go to Sydney, and catch the train from there?'

I was not looking at Philanderer, but I felt that the shaft about Sydney had gone home. I wasn't in a very generous mood. Frankly, I resented being used as an accomplice in a not so subtle attempt to suborn my pupil.

It was about time for us to leave. Stubbing his cigar in a crystal ashtray, His Honour lightly shrugged his shoulders and nonchalantly remarked, 'I hope you've gotten over all this nonsense about Clare. There's no reason why we can't be friends.'

To which that fool Pomfret replied, 'I intend to marry her.'

And bang went a spare set of the All England Law Reports (195 volumes), the Australian Legal Digest (48 volumes) and Halsbury's Laws of England (51 volumes)!

'You bloody fool,' I chided Pomfret when we were back in Chambers. 'You could've waited until you got the books before you told him that.'

THE PIG AND WHISTLE

Next day I regretted having teased George Philanderer so maliciously. I mean, his efforts to buy off Harry Pomfret had been admittedly clumsy, but they were no doubt made with the best of intentions. After all, he only had the welfare of his daughter Clare at heart. She was an only child and nobody could blame him if he was over-protective in her regard. I should not, I thought, have goaded him with the fact that Harry would travel via Sydney on his way to the Blue Mountains. Philanderer would no doubt now spend sleepless nights worrying about his daughter seeing Harry in Sydney, and wondering what mischief they might get up to. It had been, I concluded, a very mean trick on my part, to rub salt into poor old George's wounds.

And yet . . . One thing which had particularly attracted my attention while we were at Philanderer's club quite intrigued me. I went to my bookshelves and took down a copy of *Anson's Law of Contract (19th edition)*. This had been one of our prescribed textooks when I was at Law School. I opened the well-thumbed volume and there, exactly where I had placed it all those years ago, was a snapshot photograph of George Philanderer and myself and the two girls with the show-bags. Very carefully I inspected the photo of George, and was more than a little puzzled by what I saw. I took a magnifying glass (a concession to advancing middle age) from a drawer of my desk and studied the print very closely. There was no mistake about it . . . How very curious . . I had never particularly noticed that signet ring at the time.

I replaced the snapshot, put *Anson* back on the shelf, and was plunged in thought. Then I shrugged—my suspicions were unworthy. George had given me his solemn assurance . . .

Pomfret in fact left for the Blue Mountains earlier than I had told Philanderer. There was nothing much doing in the Courts during the few days before Christmas, so I gave him an early mark. As things turned out, it was lucky I did. Had he adhered to our original timetable, his trip would have been in vain.

Gerard was driving to Sydney for the holidays and Harry went with him. Before they left, Amy reminded Gerard to make sure to wear his St Christopher medal, what with all those accidents on the road, but he very smugly informed her that St Christopher had now been decanonized and was just plain *Mr* Christopher. Gerard can be very thoughtless at times. I mean, fancy telling Amy that the Sacred Heart picture in our bedroom was anatomically incorrect, and then giving her a lecture on aortas and ventricles and arteriosclerosis . . . Just showing off his poor little fund of medical knowledge, without any regard for his mother's feelings. But Amy got her subtle revenge on him, bless her. When Gerard lost his wristwatch she refused to pray to St Anthony to help him find it, and he never did.

On the way to Sydney Gerard and Harry diverged to travel along the Olympic Highway, through Wagga Wagga and Junee, until they joined the Great Western Highway, and then on to the Blue Mountains. They had no trouble in finding the Pig and Whistle, just off the Highway, so Gerard dropped Pomfret there and they arranged to meet again in Sydney the following day.

It was a very old weatherboard pub, rather run-down, with the paint peeling from a faded sign over the front door:

PIG AND WHISTLE
Tessie O'Twiddle. Prop.
Licensed to sell fermented
and spirituous liquors

Mrs O'Twiddle was a goitrous-eyed widow, henna-haired, with watermelon bosoms which she rested comfortably on the bar as she told Harry yes, she did have a room vacant, dear, just for the one night? Breakfast would be at eight o'clock, she would just get the register for him to sign, dear, would he like a drink while he was waiting?

The bar was empty save for two ancients sitting on a bench

in the corner, waiting for God, and in the meantime toothlessly muttering and mumbling to one another.

There was some considerable confusion when Harry ordered a beer. A beer? What size, dear? It appeared that Harry was uninitiated into the New South Welsh mysteries of a lady's waist, a pony, a middy, a schooner and a pot.

'Where do you come from?' Mrs O'Twiddle enquired.

'Melbourne.'

'Well, a pony for you dear,' she decided, and then enquired, 'New or Old?'

Rather than enter upon a further protracted display of ignorance of north-of-the border drinking habits, he cut his losses and ventured, 'New.'

'. . . She had five tits, that's something you don't often see,' quavered a voice from the bench in the corner.

Mrs O'Twiddle put a pony in front of Harry and went off to fetch the register.

'I've seen some things in my time,' the corner voice quavered on, 'and what I haven't seen I've touched.'

Harry tested his drink and pulled a wry face. Perhaps he should have asked for Old. He took another sip and grimaced again. They can say what they like about the water in the River Yarra, but it does make the best brew in Australia, and Harry was now learning that New South Welsh beer is a very poor substitute.

'. . . when they opened her up, they found she was riddled, just riddled,' announced a tremulous voice.

Mrs O'Twiddle returned with the register which she set down on the bar in front of Harry. 'Write the date and your name on the next line, dear, and sign it.'

'. . . riddled with it . . .'

He picked up the pen she had placed on the book. 'I suppose you get a lot of people staying here,' he remarked, idly flicking the pages. 'How far back does this book go?'

'Oh years and years,' she replied.

'. . . riddled through and through . . .'

He found the front page: 2nd October, 1962.

'. . . riddled . . .'

I'm interested in the history of the district,' Harry went on, 'I belong to the Historical Society. I'm especially interested in

Fermented and spirituous liquors

the year 1956, what sort of people used to visit the Mountains then.'

'. . . just riddled . . .'

Mrs O'Twiddle looked at him with some respect.

'I don't suppose you have the old Register, the one before this book?' he went on.

'. . . the Doctor said he'd never seen anyone so riddled . . . '

'Well I imagine it's somewhere around,' she replied. 'I'd have to look for it. But I can't leave the bar at the moment.' She gazed thoughtfully and calculatingly at Harry, then flashed him a sudden attempt at a winsome smile. 'I could hunt it out after I close the bar tonight, and bring it to your room for you.' She gave him that meaningful look which always worked wonders with overnight travelling salesmen.

'. . . so they sewed her up again . . .'

'I'd be obliged. I could wait in the bar, if you like,' Harry suggested.

'That's against the Licensing laws,' she countered. 'It might take a while to find anyway. I'll bring it to your room.' Mrs O'Twiddle was well aware of the value of a *quid pro quo*.

'. . . you'd think they'd know the difference between tonsils and testicles . . .'

Harry finished his drink and escaped. A frail, quavering voice followed him: '. . . the solicitor says he's got a good case against the hospital . . .'

For the rest of the day Harry explored the scenic wonders of the Blue Mountains, gazing spellbound across those great valleys surrounded by ancient sandstone precipices basking starkly in the sunlight, while far down below stretched expanse after expanse of dense forest, the tops of the trees forming an unending green carpet as far as the eye could see. He found a waterfall, its sudden plunge fringed with fine misty spray in its downward drop straight into the gorge, until it was lost from sight.

He must have walked for several hours, the stillness broken only by the call of the bell birds, the song of the magpies, the cheerful laughter of families of kookaburras, and the raucous prattling of the black cockatoos. He stopped a while to watch the robin redbreasts searching for food in the crumpled stumps of fallen trees, and the gang-gangs, so spectacularly coloured in their red and mottled-grey plumage, quietly feasting on the berries of a geebung.

As he walked, he came across the gaily ornamented Palais de Dance of a satin bower bird, and stood motionless to watch the cock bird's courting display in his blue bedecked bower, going through a Fred Astaire repertoire of dance routines, under the critical eye of an audience of one very attentive hen-bird.

It began to grow dark and already the evening mists of the mountains were beginning to rise. Reluctantly Harry set off for the Pig and Whistle, curiously refreshed by the quiet restfulness of this undisturbed bushland. He wondered if his mother and his unknown father had walked that way some twenty-five years before. He was tempted to stay on for a few days: he had a phone number in Sydney where he could leave a message for Gerard, and Clare was not yet aware that he was coming. He had wanted to surprise her.

Later in the evening, Harry went back to the bar, which was now chock-a-block. The two gummy old senior citizens were still in their corner, but their muttering and mumbling was lost under the swelling sound of the Mountains men at play. The Pig and Whistle had become, in its declining years, the haunt of workers for the local Council and on the Railway line—labouring men all, with a tremendous zest for noisy drinking. They laughed fit to burst their lungs, they swore like the rumble of thunder, they called boisterously to one another from across the entire length of the bar-room, they held confidential snatches of conversation from a distance of seven metres and more. Most wore faded navy singlets, and all were missing at least one front tooth, some minus four and five or more, with no replacements. Indeed, Harry and Mrs O'Twiddle were the only two people there with a full set of front teeth—and even hers came out at night.

As Harry fronted the bar to order a drink, Mrs O'Twiddle gave him what would have been, when she was twenty-five years younger, a slinky seductive look. Now she achieved no better than a lewd and pornographic grin. 'I found the old register, dear,' she said, placing before him a pony of New. "I'll bring it to your room after I close the bar,' and the grin broadened into a lascivious promise of wonderful things to come.

Harry was suddenly conscious of all eyes gazing in some

surprise, and with some suspicion, at his pony of beer. Nobody else in the bar held anything but a schooner or a pot. Hard workers, hard players, hard drinkers, they were happy in their own company these men, gregarious, jovial—shy of outsiders. The presence of a stranger among them, drinking beer out of a silly little glass, made them uneasy. They felt that they were being watched by alien eyes. They had only one defence—Harry suddenly became invisible. His presence was completely ignored. The heavy laughter, the shouting, the confusion of sound increased. There was a continual movement as they wandered around the bar talking to friends, small groups forming, dissolving, and reforming, like the wildlife in a globule of creek water seen under a microscope.

Old Cec had brought along his squeeze-box, as every so often he did, and, sitting on a stool near the bar, he began to play. His repertoire comprised old-time songs and bush ballads: *Tooral-aye-ooral-aye-addity, The Shearer's Dream of Home, If I had the Wings of an Angel Over these Prison Walls I would Fly* . . . Nobody sang, but they all listened. Two half-boozed, middle-aged rough-heads began to dance together—a country sort of dance, arms hooked, clumsily circling this way, change arms, change direction, circle back the other way, while their mates clapped time. Goodwill lay heavy on the air. Everyone was everyone's friend. Harry was captivated by the guilelessness of these simple men and their simple pleasures.

A slight altercation occurred. One of the drinkers had passed some remark which offended his fellow, who showed his displeasure by spitting in the other one's beer. A punch was thrown, returned, and suddenly it was on for young and old, on for one and all. Nobody took sides, they just fought. Now everyone was everyone's enemy. Great strong arms swung wildly, fists thudded, boots kicked, bar-stools were thrown. Crash went a window. Crash went another, then a row of spirits bottles behind the bar. The Mountains men were enjoying every bone-crunching moment of it. Schooners and pots hurtled through the air, bodies too. Harry took refuge under a table while the battle raged on, mighty oaths rending the air above the thud of fists and the smashing of glass and furniture.

Thinking that he had better get out of there as quickly as he could, Harry popped his head up above the edge of the table to reconnoitre. He was immediately struck on the forehead by a flying bar-stool and knocked unconscious . . .

When he came to, and looked groggily around him, a scene of utter desolation met his eyes. Every window was shattered, the entire stock behind the bar was destroyed, not a bar-stool remained intact. There were bodies heaped everywhere, some unconscious, some groaning, blood, beer, glass, complete devastation. The calm after the hurricane.

The bar doors swung open, and in strode the local sergeant, a big man, bulging in his too-tight uniform.

'All right,' he bellowed, 'Who started all this?'

Up from behind the bar now gradually appeared first the henna hair, then the goitrous eyes, then the ill-fitting dentures, and then the watermelon bosoms of the landlady of the Pig and Whistle.

'Who started it all?' demanded the sergeant in a stern, authoritarian voice.

Mrs O'Twiddle looked helplessly around the bar, at the corpses of her customers, at the broken windows, the wrecked furniture.

'Who was it?' repeated the arm of the law.

Mrs O'Twiddle's fearful eyes lighted on a sacrificial lamb, still barely conscious and blinking uncomprehendingly at this aftermath of the Battle of Armageddon. 'Him,' she said, and pointed at Harry.

The cell in which young Pomfret spent the night lacked all mod cons and was more than a little overcrowded. His cellmates were an exclusive band of drunk and disorderlies who contentedly snored themselves sober the long night through.

In the morning they were all unceremoniously dragged before the local Magistrate.

Harry felt decidedly unwell. There was dried blood on his forehead and where it had trickled down around his eyes and clogged his eyebrows. After a night in the cells his clothes were dirty and crumpled. He looked no better than the rest of the overnight riff-raff. His name was called and he was hustled into Court by a young policeman who led him towards the Bench.

'Harry Pomfret,' read the Clerk of Courts perfunctorily and at a great speed, 'you are charged that on the 22nd day of December you were found drunk and disorderly in a public place, to wit, the Pig and Whistle Hotel. How do you plead, guilty or not guilty?'

'Not guilty,' Harry replied, thereby creating judicial history. In that bailiwick, nobody had ever contested a drunk and disorderly charge in living memory.

The Sergeant went into the witness box. 'Your Worship,' he recited in a flat voice, tonelessly, like the race-caller at Rosehill, 'last night, as a result of something I was told, I attended the Pig and Whistle Hotel where I saw the defendant lying on the floor. I could smell alcohol on his breath and he was unsteady on his feet. His clothing was disarranged. I arrested the defendant.'

It is a commonplace in our profession that the lawyer who acts for himself has a fool for his client. None the less Pomfret, still wet behind the ears, decided to cross-examine the witness on his own behalf. He soon discovered one of the harsh facts of life: Barristers often get away with blue murder in the type of questions they ask, unchallenged, but when John Citizen tries to do the same thing for himself, it is a very different and very sad story.

'Were there any other people in the bar?' he began.

'The Court is not interested in what other people were doing, only in what *you* were doing,' interrupted the Magistrate tersely.

Harry tried again; 'Had there been a fight in the bar?'

'You are not charged with assault,' the Magistrate once more interrupted. 'You are charged with being drunk and disorderly. Don't ask irrelevant questions.'

'But Your Worship, I only wanted to establish—'

'You are not entitled at this stage of the proceedings to make a statement. Only to ask questions. Is there anything else you want to ask the Sergeant?'

Harry swallowed, ground his teeth, and enquired, 'Had I sustained a head injury?'

'Yes,' replied the Sergeant, 'a cut to the forehead.'

The Magistrate took up the running: 'Was that injury consistent with the defendant falling down when drunk, Sergeant?'

'Yes, Your Worship,' the policeman very willingly agreed.

'Does he live locally?'

'No, Your Worship. He comes from Melbourne, I believe.'

'We don't want outsiders coming up to the Mountains and giving the place a bad name, do we?'

'No, Your Worship,' the Sergeant hastened to agree.

'The defendant will be convicted and—'

'I want to give evidence,' Harry said at the top of his voice.

'Very well, go into the witness box,' the Magistrate was in a hurry to finish his cases and then go and play golf. 'Swear the witness,' he rapped out, to the Bench Clerk.

So the formalities began. Harry was asked his name . . . his address . . . his occupation—

'Barrister-at-law,' he replied.

There was a sudden, startled silence. Everyone in the Court temporarily stopped breathing. The clock on the wall stopped ticking. The magistrate hurriedly scribbled a note, passed it to his Bench Clerk, who passed it to the policeman on duty, who passed it to the prosecuting Sergeant, who read it, and nodded to the Magistrate.

'I suppose,' the Magistrate said to Harry, now in a most conciliatory tone, 'that your evidence is that this is a case of mistaken identity.'

Harry, who was intending to say no such thing, at least had the wit to agree: 'Yes.'

'That could well be so, I suppose, Sergeant?' the Magistrate enquired anxiously.

'Yes, Your Worship,' the policeman agreed. 'Very easily mistaken.'

'Under those circumstances, of course, the Information will be dismissed. You are free to leave, Mr Pomfret.'

And they whisked him out of Court more quickly than they had whisked him in. They even drove him back, passenger in the police motor-cycle-and-sidecar, to Mrs O'Twiddle's licensed hostelry.

'I couldn't dob in one of my regular customers, dear, could I?' she explained as she pulled a beer for him. 'Anyway, I've got the old Register for you.' She took it out from under the bar and placed it before Harry.

Eagerly he turned the pages to June, 1956 and perused the entries. Sure enough, exactly as I had predicted, a Mr and Mrs John Smith had stayed at the hotel over the Queen's Birthday weekend. He examined the handwriting carefully, but could not decide which of the two judges' signatures it most resembled. The script was fairly large, like that of Sir Anthony Opscotch. But the letters were cramped together, like Mr Justice Cumquat's. He frowned, in puzzlement.

'Did you find what you wanted, dear?' she asked.

He nodded. Mrs O'Twiddle was busy connecting a new barrel of beer to one of the taps at the bar. There was a loud hiss of escaping gas. Under cover of the noise, Harry surreptitiously tore out the page, swiftly folded it, and placed it in his pocket.

Then he collected his belongings from his room, paid the account—'You needn't really,' she said, but he insisted—and walked to the railway station, to catch the next train for Sydney. He had to wait for several hours, and was exhausted, after his sleepless night in the cells, but he was too excited to nod off. He kept taking the page out of his pocket, scrutinizing his father's handwriting, refolding the page and placing it back in his pocket, then taking it out again, scrutinizing it once more . . .

At last the train arrived, and Harry fell into a deep sleep for the next two hours, oblivious of the great rocky crags, the deep gorges, the sheer cliffs and the breath-taking valleys that filed past the train windows as it diddle-de-dum, diddle-de-dee'd its way down the mountain passes and then across the Emu Plains towards Sydney.

He had only just been in time. That very night, the Pig and Whistle Hotel was burned to the ground. The Police suspected foul play and the Arson Squad was called in. They concluded that the fire had been deliberately lit, for they found several newspapers, recent copies of the Melbourne Herald, which had apparently been doused in kerosene, and which crumbled to black powder at the touch.

THWARTED LOVE AND UNBRIDLED PASSION

When Pomfret arrived on Gerard's doorstep, still sporting his wounds of the battle at the Pig and Whistle, Gerard bathed and bandaged his forehead, gave him a sleeping draught and told him to rest. Pomfret promptly collapsed on to a day-bed and did not wake up until almost noon the following day. By which time, of course, Gerard was already sensuously stretched out in the sun, on the sands of Bondi Beach, slavering at the mouth at the sight of so many suntanned surf-sprayed sea goddesses, and singling out a suitable specimen to add to his collection.

Harry phoned Prince of Wales Hospital.

'I'm sorry, sir, Miss Philanderer is on holidays over the Christmas break,' the switchboard girl informed him. 'Can I take a message?'

He phoned Clare's apartment. No answer.

Having sighted his quarry, Gerard stood up, shook the sand from his towel, and waved an arm at the ice-cream boy, who came stumbling across the beach. Then, nonchalantly swinging his towel in one hand, and carefully holding an ice-cream cone in the other, Gerard walked casually towards where a young girl in a skimpy bikini was asleep on the sand.

Harry telephoned a taxi and was almost immediately on his way to Clare's flat. He had wanted to give her a pleasant surprise by arriving unexpectedly in Sydney, but now he was uncertain, in fact quite apprehensive. What if Clare had gone to Melbourne, to surprise *him?*.

As Gerard drew closer to the sleeping girl, he was more than satisfied with his choice. Bronzed by the sun, she wore a little paper shield over her nose to protect it from burning. Her long hair, still damp from the surf, spread across the rolled-up towel which served as a pillow.

When he reached her, Gerard stopped, took aim, turned his ice-cream cone upside down, and dropped it on her navel.

The girl screamed and sat bolt upright, in astonishment and alarm.

Nobody answered the door when Harry rang the bell of Clare's apartment. He rang again. Three times. Then he enquired at the next-door apartment.

'She's gone away,' the neighbour said. 'She left this morning. Her father called for her. He had just arrived from Melbourne.'

Carefully cleaning up the ice-cream with one end of his towel, and now on his knees beside her, Gerard apologized profusely, 'That was very clumsy of me.'

The beach-girl said nothing. She was too bewildered.

'Do you know where they've gone?' Harry enquired.

'Not really,' the neighbour replied. 'Somewhere down the South Coast, but that's not much help.'

'Are they going by train?' Harry asked, hoping perhaps to catch Clare at Central Station.

'By car. Her father had driven from Melbourne. He stayed overnight in the Blue Mountains and arrived here just after breakfast.'

'You'll have to go back into the surf,' Gerard decided, 'or you'll be all sticky from the ice-cream. Come on.' And he took the girl's hands and drew her to her feet. She had by now somewhat recovered her composure, and was smiling uncertainly at him.

'Do you know how long she'll be away?' Harry asked.

The neighbour shook her head, 'She didn't say. Probably until some time in January. Do you want to leave a message?'

'Tell her Harry called.'

'Are you Harry?' the neighbour exclaimed. 'You really are a rat-fink! She was waiting and waiting to hear from you right up to the minute she left. Why didn't you phone?'

Meanwhile, cavorting with his new-found playmate in the tumbling breakers of the broiling surf, Gerard went through a well-rehearsed routine which was not only scandalous, considering that there were several thousand people out there on the beach, but also, considering the size and strength of the waves, almost physically impossible. Still, as they say, love will always find a way.

During the next few days Harry waited on, disconsolately,

hoping against hope that a miracle might happen, that he might hear from Clare. He went to look at the Opera House and the Harbour Bridge. He went to look at the animals at Taronga Park and the naked people on Lady Jane Beach. He went for a ride on the Manly ferry and a walk through the Botanic Gardens. He visited the Art Gallery, the Australian Museum, Pinchgut Island and Observatory Hill. But his heart was not in it. If ever there was an unhappy tourist, trudging from one scenic splendour to another, it was Harry Pomfret.

He saw little of Gerard, who was by now totally absorbed in his wonderful new erotic escapade. Just occasionally Gerard would surface, looking very haggard, racing into his apartment for a clean change of clothing, drinking three quick cups of very black coffee, and then was gone in a flash, back for more punishment.

Finally Harry could stand the loneliness and the frustration of his Sydney misadventure no longer, and caught a plane back to Melbourne. Just before he boarded the aircraft, he again phoned Clare's apartment, in a last hopeless gesture of despair. Still no answer.

It was unfortunate that he did not wait for just one more buzz on the phone, before he hung up, because Clare had at that very moment walked through her front door. She ran to the phone: nothing but dial-tone. She waited, wondering. She waited in vain. Harry was already fastening his seat belt.

Clare's holiday on the South Coast had been cut short because her father had to return to Melbourne in time for the announcement of the New Year's Honours list. All his friends, and most of his enemies, would be eager to congratulate him on his knighthood, and George Philanderer wanted to be there to wallow in the glory of it all.

Amy and I were holidaying at a rented beach house, down on the Peninsula, when I read his name in the Honours List in the *AGE*. So, of course, I wrote him the usual note, appropriate for such occasions: 'Heartiest congratulations . . . well-merited . . . distinguished citizen . . . etc.' and posted it without a stamp. George wouldn't mind paying the postage, I reckoned, and the penalty postage too, for another letter to add to his scrap-album.

Several days later I received a desperate message from a solicitor: Would I make an urgent application to the Judge in

Chambers to obtain bail for a special client of his? The client certainly was special: I had twice before *almost* got him off on assault with a weapon charges, and had also, with a similar conspicuous lack of success, defended him on burglary and warehouse-breaking charges.

Time was when, apart from such trivial punishments as the hacking off of ears and splitting and burning the nostrils for forgery, convicted persons were branded: M on the right hand for manslaughter, T on the left hand for theft, F on either cheek for felony, B on the forehead for blasphemy. Vagabonds who would not work (the 'dole-bludgers' of those days) were **marked with a whott iron in the brest with the mark of** V and were sentenced to work for two years. If they tried to run away from this enforced slavery, they were then branded **on the forhed or the ball of the cheke with a hote iron with the signe of an** S.

If these amusing customs had not fallen into disuse, my villainous client would have looked like a mangled bowl of alphabet soup. Now here he was again, this time on a murder rap, and according to the police, he had confessed all. The chances of him being granted bail, whilst awaiting trial, were practically zero.

To make matters worse, the Judge in Chambers was Mr Justice Cumquat and he was sure to be in a surly mood. The Supreme Court closes down, lock, stock and barrel, from mid-December to early February, save for one unfortunate judge, no doubt chosen by drawing straws, who has to stay behind to make sure nobody steals the Statue of Justice, and to deal with any urgent matters which cannot await the return of the other judges from their happy holiday-making. This solitary judge only sits one day a week, but Cumquat would be certain to be eaten with envy of his more fortunate brother judges, and in consequence his temper would be frayed, his comments snappy, his co-operation minimal, and his whole demeanour sufficient to strike terror into the heart of any Counsel who made an application which His Honour did not consider sufficiently important to prevent him also from going on vacation.

The solicitor assured me: 'My client needs bail so that he can earn enough money to pay for his defence at the trial.' My earlier experiences with that particular client would have led me to believe that his method of earning money was confined to

Burglary and other larcenies

burglary and other larcenies great and small. Still, business is business, so I travelled back to Chambers, leaving Amy to concoct some indigestible recipe to welcome my return, bless her.

'Your horoscope in this morning's paper says that a long journey will lead to a disappointment,' she warned me, just before I drove off.

Her forebodings were correct: Mr Justice Cumquat snarlingly refused my application for bail. This he did in thirty seconds flat, and then spent the next fourteen and a half minutes upbraiding me for bringing such an unimportant and trivial matter before the court, until I rather lost my sense of discretion.

'Trivial, Y'r Honour?' I smiled blandly. 'The liberty of the subject?'

So then he went on squeaking for another fourteen and a half minutes about the respect due to the Bench by Counsel, while I stood, meekly muttering, 'Yes, Y'r Honour . . . No Y'r Honour . . . Yes, Y'r Honour . . . No, Y'r Honour . . . '

'Rotten little runt!' I growled as I returned to Chambers, and then to Pomfret, who was researching a list of cases for a difficult Opinion I had to write: 'If Mr Bloody Justice Cumquat is your father, you've got nothing going for you.'

I picked up a letter on my desk. It was a reply from Sir George Philanderer, thanking me for my letter of congratulations.

'I saw the Register Book of the Pig and Whistle,' Pomfret said, triumphantly holding out the page for my inspection, together with the photostats of the two judges' signatures.

I compared the handwriting. 'It is a bold sweeping hand, like Sir Anthony Opscotch's,' I commented, 'but there again, the characters are inclined to be cramped together like Cumquat's.'

'Whose do you think it is?' Pomfret asked.

Again I considered: 'On the whole I would plummet for Opscotch,' I replied. 'He probably had to cramp the words together to fit them in the space provided, and the capitals were no doubt a fancy attempt to disguise his handwriting . . . Yes,' I concluded, 'it seems almost certain that Sir Anthony is your sire. Congratulations! He is a very respectable sort of father for anyone to have. A bit eccentric perhaps, the way he takes that three-legged dog with him wherever he goes, even into Court, but none the less a worthy progenitor for an up-and-coming young barrister.'

'Shall I write him a letter, do you think?' Pomfret asked.

'No! No letters!' I exclaimed in alarm. 'Remember what happened to Applebaum after you sent him a letter—Went off his head. No letters!'

'Well, what then?'

'Just give me time to think about that. I'll sort it all out. Just leave it to me,' I reassured him. Then to change the subject, I enquired, 'How was Clare?'

'I didn't see her,' Pomfret replied, and told me his sad story.

'You should have stayed an extra few days in Sydney,' I informed him. 'Her father is well and truly back in Melbourne.' And I held up Philanderer's note which lay on my desk.

Pomfret was thunderstruck, quite crestfallen.

'Why don't you go back to Sydney for a few days,' I advised him. 'Gerard is still there. You could stay with him.'

'Thank you,' he stammered, 'but I . . .I. . .I can't afford the plane fare.'

I looked at him quizzically, then remarked, 'It so happens that there are some original documents in the archives of the Mitchell Library in Sydney that I would like you to have a look at, for the purposes of the Opinion you have been working on. Arthur will arrange your plane ticket there and back, and all other necessary travelling expenses. Can you leave this afternoon?'

Pomfret's jaw dropped. He couldn't find the words to reply.

'Go home and pack,' I went on, 'I'll leave on your desk a list of the references I want you to look up, so don't forget to collect it before you go. And get your ticket and expenses from Arthur. Off you go.'

Still lost for words, Pomfret went to the door.

'And I don't want to see you back here before this time next week,' I called after him.

I picked up the page from the Register of the Pig and Whistle and again examined it. As I replaced the page on my desk, it lay beside the note Philanderer had just written to me. Some similarity caught my eye and I picked up both pieces of paper and compared them carefully . . . very odd . . . The *Mr and Mrs John Smith* was more like George Philanderer's handwriting than that of Opscotch or Cumquat!

Still, it had been written more than 25 years ago, and people's handwritings do change, and anyway Philanderer had assured me he was not Pomfret's father . . . Still, it was very odd.

I took down *Anson's Law of Contract (19th edition)* from my bookshelves, extracted that photo of George and me and the two girls with the show bags, and again examined it attentively. There was no doubt George was wearing a signet ring. I cast my mind back to my conversation with Philanderer, to see whether there was any ambiguity about the way he had denied all knowledge of Pomfret's parentage. But no, his denial had been quite categoric, without any shadow of doubt.

Meanwhile, in Sydney, Clare's neighbour had told her that Harry had called, and had left the phone number of Gerard's rented flat. Clare rang there about a hundred times before she finally got a reply.

'He's gone back to Melbourne,' Gerard croaked in a very husky and debilitated voice. 'He waited and waited, but in the end gave up all hope.'

Clare decided there was only one thing to be done. She packed a suitcase, phoned T.A.A., and left for the airport.

Her plane, en route for Melbourne, passed Harry's plane, en route for Sydney, as they each flew over the Snowy River Hydro-Electric generating station at Adaminaby.

On arrival in Melbourne, Clare immediately phoned Harry. No answer. She tried to phone me but I was by then back at the holiday beach house on the Peninsula, with Amy. So then she rang my clerk.

'Oh, Mr Pomfret's in Sydney, Miss,' Arthur informed her. 'He left this morning.'

In the meantime, in Sydney, receiving no answer to his phone calls to Clare's apartment, Harry called there in person, only to be told by the next-door neighbour that Clare had gone to Melbourne that very day, to see him.

Two hours later, just as Clare was boarding a T.A.A. flight in Melbourne, Harry was boarding an Ansett flight in Sydney. And once again, their planes passed in mid-air, this time ten miles west of Burrinjuck Dam.

So for the next fortnight Harry sat solitary and glum in my Chambers, looking up cases for the Opinion I had to write, and wondering how he would explain to me, when I returned, why he had not researched the documents in the Mitchell Library.

BOOM! AND FAREWELL

When I finally did return, I found that I had been briefed to appear in a case which concerned a dispute over a Will, so I was too preoccupied preparing my cross-examination to pay any attention to Harry Pomfret and his thwarted love-life. As I glanced through the papers in the brief I noticed that Sir Anthony Opscotch was to be the trial judge.

I then and there determined that young Pomfret must be with me in Court during that trial: There is no better way of gauging a judge's measure then to watch how he comports himself in Court. No other member of the community receives such an ostentatious display of subservience, being bowed to, being deferred to, as he sits up there on his judicial throne, and this extravagant flattery can bring out the best and the worst in his nature. If he is a man of infinite compassion, it shines through like a clear light. If he is by nature a bully, this also shows just as surely. It is a gruelling test for the character of a lesser man.

But Opscotch was not a lesser man. Weathering the storm of day to day life with eleven giggling daughters had seen to that. Just getting into the bathroom of a morning was a battle of wits, and then fighting his way through all those bottles and sachets and pressure-packs and jars and tubes of moisturizing cream, skin lotion, eye-shadow, hair softener, hair spray, nourishing cream, nail polish, indeed the whole multitudinous range of Coty, Revlon, Max Factor and Helena Rubinstein beauty preparations, had endowed him with the gift of true humility. Infinitely patient, a twinkle in his eye, never so happy as when he was shut up in his library with his books, the three-legged dog asleep at his feet; never so happy as when he was out sailing his yacht over the wide blue waters of Port Phillip Bay; never so happy as when he listened day after day to Counsel's dry and weighty arguments on some intricate point of law – I was certain that my pupil would be proud to be a son of such a man, so at peace with all the world. And this trial would provide Pomfret with an opportunity to know and understand his father.

'If he is my father . . . ' Harry faltered.

'There can be no doubt about it,' I reassured him, 'no doubt whatsoever. Not now that we've seen that page from the hotel Register. You should congratulate yourself that your search has ended so successfully. Being the son of Sir Anthony Opscotch is quite a feather in your cap.'

'He hasn't said he is my father yet,' Pomfret remarked hesitantly.

'Leave all that to me,' I countered enthusiastically. 'I shall arrange a meeting and settle this matter once and forever.'

But for the moment it was back to the grind of earning a living, and I pondered and pondered over how best I should go about cross-examining Griselda Hargelmarsch.

Griselda Hargelmarsch was a solid lump of a woman, with thick arms, thick legs and a thick neck. She had been a nursing sister and her powerful biceps bore witness to many years spent slapping the sick. Her short-cut hair, her protruding jaw and her implacable green eyes made her a force to be reckoned with.

Griselda had the good fortune to be the beneficiary and executrix of her old aunt's Will. The aunt had died possessed of a Victorian mansion in Kew, and a very sizeable bank balance. Griselda had not seen the old lady for ages, but as she was the only living relative, she copped the lot. Subject to certain provisos:

The old aunt had, in her declining years, taken into her home a destitute female, by way of companion. This bird-like creature, a Miss Possell, had fetched and carried, cleaned and polished, cooked and scrubbed, and kept the Victorian mansion in spick-and-span order, for which devoted service the old aunt had left her a legacy of $400.

The only other inhabitant of the mansion was a black and white alley cat named Brandy Snaps, who had arrived uninvited, stayed on, and wormed his way into the old aunt's affections. So assiduous had Brandy Snaps been in his cunning attentions, that his mistress had made special provision for him in her Will.

Everything, except Miss Possell's $400, was left to Griselda, true enough. But for so long as Brandy Snaps might live, the Victorian mansion with its antique furniture was to be used as a home for the cat, and the income from the money in the bank was to be disbursed for his care and welfare, including a retainer for Miss Possell to look after him. So Miss Possell had a vested interest in Brandy Snaps, for, during his lifetime, she had the run of a most comfortable home, and an assured income.

Griselda, on the other hand, had a vested interest in Brandy Snaps' early demise. She had no choice, as executrix, but to leave the cat and Miss Possell in possession of the Victorian mansion, and she regularly and reluctantly paid over the income from the bank account. Still, the thought of that wretched animal sitting on silk cushions and eating the best barramundi, and keeping her out of her inheritance, made Griselda grind her teeth in exasperation and fury. And the knowledge that Brandy Snaps was still only a young cat, and a very healthy young cat at that, lit the fires of hell in her soul.

One morning, while Brandy Snaps was sunning himself on the front verandah, Griselda arrived, carrying a hessian chaff-bag. 'Here, puss, puss, puss,' she cooed as she gently picked him up, dumped him in the bag, and tied the top with binder-twine. Then she marched into the house, straight to the bathroom, where she locked the door, filled the bath with water, and plonked the chaff-bag—and the cat—in the bath.

The Victorian mansion was immediately rent by horrible gurgling screams of the unfortunate Brandy Snaps, while Miss Possell, in hysterics, tearfully banged at the bathroom door. In vain. An hour passed while Griselda stood watch over the bath, holding the chaff-bag under water with a plastic bath-stool, until the wails at last subsided, and the chaff-bag struggled no more.

Then, and only then, did Griselda emerge. Before the terrified eyes of Miss Possell, she undid the binder-twine, emptied a very damp and very dead Brandy Snaps out on to the hall floor, and said, 'Now, pack your bags, and get out!'

But Miss Possell did not get out. She refused to budge. So Griselda consulted her solicitor who commenced Supreme Court proceedings by way of a Writ for possession of the premises and for the ejectment of Miss Possell, seeking injunctions to restrain her from being in and remaining on the aforesaid premises.

I was delivered a brief to appear for Miss Possell at the trial, and was more than a little nonplussed. 'The trouble is,' I explained 'you were only entitled to remain in the house and to receive the income from the moneys in the bank while Brandy Snaps was alive.'

'But—' began Miss Possell.

'Griselda killed the cat,' Miss Possell's solicitor interrupted, 'Contrary to the clear intentions of her aunt's Will.'

'But—' Miss Possell began again.

'Except for the legacy of $400, the aunt left all her possessions to Griselda,' I pointed out, 'and that included the cat. Griselda became in fact the owner of the cat.'

'But—' Miss Possell tried once more.

'If Griselda wants to drown her own cat,' I went on, 'there is no law against it.'

'But—' Miss Possell's frail little voice was determined to be heard.

'The Will said nothing about making sure the cat stayed alive, only that Griselda had to leave it in undisturbed possession of the house while it lived.'

'But—'

'Yes, what is it, Miss Possell?' I asked, impatiently.

'But Brandy Snaps isn't dead,' she said.

There was a sudden silence.

'Not dead?' I asked. 'I thought you said Griselda drowned him.'

'After Griselda left, Brandy Snaps revived, and he's still there,' Miss Possell explained.

I narrowed my eyes and considered. Miss Possell was one of those little old ladies who wouldn't harm a fly, but I have been long enough around the Law Courts to know that little old ladies who wouldn't harm a fly are the most proficient perjurers ever to enter a witness box. In their frail little voices they tell the most outrageous lies, unblinking, and because they remind everyone of their mother, they are always believed. I had no doubt whatsoever that Miss Possell had done a quick round of all the pet shops until she found a suitable black and white replacement, who was now at this very moment sitting on silk cushions, munching mullet.

However, I pushed these misgivings to one side. Professional ethics preclude a barrister from disbelieving his own client. If

Miss Possell said Brandy Snaps was still alive, that was the end of the matter. I just had to accept the fact as true, whatever my own thoughts on the subject.

The great day arrived. 'All stand!' bellowed the tipstaff to herald Mr Justice Opscotch's entry into the Court. As His Honour sat, he cast a glance beside him, to make sure that his three-legged dog was comfortably ensconced in its own special chair.

Griselda was a formidable witness. Very unashamed and matter-of-fact she described how she had drowned Brandy Snaps in the bath, and by her mien defied anybody to challenge her right to do so.

I rose to cross-examine. 'Did you not consider it contrary to your aunt's wishes, to drown her cat?' I began.

'Aunt didn't say I had to keep it alive, just to provide for it while it lived,' she answered squarely, not even glancing at me.

'Are you sure you drowned Brandy Snaps?' I continued.

'By the time I'd finished with that cat, it was well and truly dead,' Griselda snapped.

'Did you test its pulse?' Opscotch cracked a judicial funny, at which we all dutifully tittered.

But Griselda was not to be put off by some old judge's feeble quips. 'I've drowned plenty of cats in my time,' she retorted grumpily, 'and this one was no exception.'

I had the distinct feeling that Opscotch did not like Griselda, did not like her at all, but the law is the law, and if she had the law on her side, then he would have to decide in her favour.

'Have you ever heard the saying that a cat has nine lives?' I asked her.

'There were none of them left by the time I'd finished with it,' she huffed.

'If I were to tell you that Brandy Snaps is alive and well, despite your attempt to drown him, what would you say?' I continued, and I noticed an amused gleam in Opscotch's eye. He had been a judge for too long not to see through my question, and he shot a shrewd, appraising look at my little old lady.

'I'd say Miss Possell has done a round of the pet shops and bought another one like it,' Griselda countered fiercely, her green eyes darting malicious daggers at me.

Then Opscotch bore in: 'How can you say that, until you have actually seen the cat? Cats don't drown easily, you know.' Enjoying the irony of the situation, he went on, 'You didn't take the cat away. You didn't bury it. You just left it there for Miss Possell to dispose of. How can you know whether it revived or not?'

Griselda bit her lip, and said nothing. She realized she had been a bit hasty in her reply.

'Now here,' I went on, turning triumphantly around to where Pomfret was sitting behind me, with a wicker cane basket at his feet, 'is Brandy Snaps himself!' I caught a twinkling, disbelieving gleam in Opscotch's eye as Pomfret handed me the basket, which I placed on the Bar table. 'You have just denied that the cat could be alive, before you even saw him. Can you deny it now?'

I opened the lid of the basket, picked up the purring pussy and placed him on the Bar table. The green malevolence of Griselda's eyes lit up like fireworks.

'It's a hoax!' she shouted, 'It's a substitute! It's a dirty trick!'

Her vehemence was so great and her voice so loud that the cat jumped in alarm from the Bar table to the Judge's Associate's desk and then up on the Bench itself, right in front of His Honour, as if seeking sanctuary, and miaowed nervously.

There was a low growl from the chair beside His Honour, and the cat miaowed again. At this, the three-legged dog stood up on his chair, placed his one front paw on the Bench and barked excitedly. The cat, at this unexpected turn of events, turned tail and ran along the full length of the Bench, followed now by a delighted yapping dog. The cat jumped from the Bench down into the well of the Court, and so did the three-legged dog, and a furious chase ensued, around and around the Court, in and out the seats reserved for the public, under the Bar table, around the witness box, back again to the public seats, while the judge banged his gavel on the bench and cried 'Order! Order!' and his Associate and his tipstaff and the policemen on duty at the Court door all joined in pursuit, and the public screamed.

At last the three-legged dog bailed up the cat in a corner, at which the cat turned, lashed out and scratched the dog on the nose. The three-legged dog uttered a tremendous wail and went for the lick of his life, now followed by an avenging screeching cat.

'Catch that cat! Catch that cat!' bellowed Opscotch, banging blue murder with his gavel, 'Catch that cat!'

Like a cowboy with a lariat

The dog, by this stage quite demoralized, ran howling in front of the seat where Pomfret was sitting, the cat hot on his heels. With great presence of mind, Pomfret leaned over and grabbed the cat by the tail, then, swinging it excitedly around his head, like a cowboy with a lariat, ran to the Court door. The policemen on duty promptly opened the door, and Pomfret, still swinging the cat, burst into the corridor, to the horror of a group of solicitors' clerks, who ran helter-skelter in the other direction.

Not quite knowing what to do, Pomfret let go of the cat's tail. The cat sailed through the air, made a perfect four-paw landing, and then zoomed out through the front entrance to the Law Courts, out on to the road, where it was immediately run over and squashed quite flat by a passing taxi.

When Pomfret returned to the Court, His Honour had succeeded in restoring order. The three-legged dog was again in its chair; Griselda was in the witness box; the public were quiet and wondering; I was standing at the Bar table; and the Judge was sitting impassive.

'Well,' said His Honour to Pomfret, 'What have you done with Brandy Snaps?'

'It's not Brandy Snaps!' growled Griselda.

'Be quiet, woman,' the Judge rebuked her firmly. 'Where is Brandy Snaps, young man?'

'He ran out on to the street and was killed by a car,' Pomfret explained lamely.

I groaned. Pomfret had done it again! Thanks to his interference, I had once more lost a perfect case just as I was on the point of winning it.

Opscotch looked at me, also in some dismay. 'That seems to settle the matter, doesn't it?' he murmured. 'If the cat is dead, I have no option but to make the order sought, for the ejectment of your client.'

I nodded dumbly.

'Of course I have a discretion on the question of costs,' Opscotch went on, 'and under all the circumstances I intend to order that Miss Possell's legal costs be paid by the Executrix of the Estate. But that is as far as I can go.'

I nodded again and murmured, 'If Y'r Honour pleases.'

'Just who is that helpful young man?' the Judge asked, drily.

'I regret to say, Y'r Honour,' I replied, 'that helpful young man is m' learned Reader, Mr Pomfret.'

Opscotch suddenly looked at Harry very fixedly, and smiled. 'I should not care to be in your shoes, Mr Pomfret, when you get back to your Master's den.'

On our way back, in painful silence, we were overtaken by Sir Anthony's tipstaff. Excusing himself, he delivered a message, 'His Honour said he would be very pleased if you and your pupil would join him for tea in his chambers.' So we retraced our steps.

Opscotch was quite effusive. 'You showed great initiative, Pomfret, in tackling that cat. You could have been badly scratched. Great initiative.' Then turning to me and with a chuckle, 'But not quite the sort of initiative you would appreciate, Dominic?'

I shrugged my shoulders deprecatingly. 'One can't win them all, Judge,' I smiled back, but in my heart I was wondering if I ever would win a case again, with Pomfret perched on my shoulder like a bird of ill-omen.

'I am very grateful for your actions, Pomfret. My dog could have been badly hurt by that cat, if you hadn't come to the rescue.' Opscotch glanced at the dog now snugly settled down in a basket in the corner of the room, and added, somewhat unnecessarily, 'He only has three legs, you know.'

We talked over tea for a few minutes, until the atmosphere became sufficiently relaxed for me to approach the topic so important to my pupil.

'My Reader was conceived at the Pig and Whistle hotel in the Blue Mountains on Queen's Birthday weekend 1956,' I said.

Opscotch looked at me, looked at Pomfret, looked at me again, looked at Pomfret again, and replied, 'Really? How very interesting.'

'His father is a Supreme Court judge,' I went on doggedly.

Again Opscotch looked at us both in turn, twice, three times. 'Really?' he said, 'How interesting.' He paused to consider, and added, 'Which judge?'

'He doesn't know,' I answered, 'but we've given that matter some thought and have come to the conclusion that it must be either you or Mr Justice Cumquat. I hope I don't offend,' I added hastily, because for one awful minute it looked as if Opscotch was about to ring for his tipstaff to throw us out.

The moment of danger passed and after an embarrassed pause Opscotch answered stiffly, 'Well I can't speak for my brother judge, of course, but I can assure you, young man, that you're no relative of mine. Never been to the Blue Mountains in my life.'

There was a long silence, none of us quite knowing what to say. The calm was at length broken by Opscotch. He began to snigger, then to chuckle, then to laugh, until finally he was rocking backwards and forwards in tremendous hearty guffaws. 'Don't know which judge is your father!' he roared explosively, 'Me or Cumquat! Well, it's not me, so you'd better ask him.' And he fell about in paroxysms of mirth.

Pomfret and I waited patiently until Opscotch had laughed himself out.

'I hope you didn't mind my asking you, Judge,' I at length remarked, 'but it seemed better to bring the matter out into the open and get a straight answer, one way or the other.'

'Quite right, Dominic, quite right.' He fell into reflective thought, and then said, 'Look, I'm much obliged to you, Pomfret, for what you did just now in Court, catching the cat and all that, and I'd be prepared to sound out Cumquat for you, if you like. Discreetly, of course.'

'I'd be very grateful,' Pomfret murmured.

'Think nothing of it, nothing of it. Consider it done. Do you chaps go fishing?' abruptly he changed the subject.

'Yes,' Pomfret replied.

'Making up a small fishing party this weekend, on my yacht. Just me and a couple of the younger judges. Would you care to join us?'

'Very willingly,' Pomfret replied.

'I'm afraid I'm not a good sailor,' I remarked. 'Always get seasick. So I had better decline.'

'Too bad, too bad,' the judge observed. 'Still, you come, Pomfret. Plenty of fish out in the Bay. Have a good time.'

Later that day, as Opscotch with his three-legged dog was ambling along one of those long, solemn, echoing, flagstoned corridors of Judges' Chambers, he met Philanderer and Cumquat, still in their scarlet and ermine, returning from a hard day's work in the Court of Appeal.

'I say, you chaps,' he challenged them, 'Guess who has a bastard son over in Barristers' Chambers?'

They stopped dead in their tracks.

'Is it you, Cumquat?' he chortled. Then maliciously, enjoying their bemusement, he added. 'Or perhaps even you, Philanderer?'

I had not mentioned Philanderer's name to Opscotch and his last remark was made out of sheer devilment. But its effect on George Philanderer was immediate. He became crimson with anger, turned on his heel, and stalked off.

Opscotch watched him go, shrugged his shoulders, and returned to the attack. 'There's a young barrister named Pomfret who claims that you are his father. Says he was conceived one Queen's Birthday weekend in the Blue Mountains, at the Pea and Thimble hotel . . .' he paused, 'or perhaps it was the Pig and Whistle . . .' he paused again, '. . . or maybe the Fife and Cymbal . . . Anyway, he is quite certain you are his father.'

Mr Justice Cumquat looked at Opscotch suspiciously.

'Come, come, learned brother,' Opscotch went on cheerily, 'why don't you set the young man's mind at rest, and own up?' With which sally, he continued on his way, the three-legged dog at his heels, leaving Cumquat eyeing his retreating back appraisingly.

On the Sunday I drove Pomfret down to the marina where Opscotch's yacht was moored. 'Seeing I can't join in, I might as well see you off,' I explained, as I unloaded Pomfret's fishing-basket from the boot of my car.

We went and watched the yacht being put in the water, and on the way back I was surprised to see Sir George Philanderer's Rolls Royce parked nearby. I was even more surprised when I caught a glimpse of Cumquat nonchalantly wandering along the shore.

'I thought His Honour said two younger judges were going with you?' I remarked to Pomfret.

'There they are,' he replied, pointing, 'Mr Justice Peewee and Mr Justice Plump.' And they were indeed there, waiting to board the yacht. (Of course the word *younger* is a comparative term and, in the case of judges, it meant that Peewee and Plump were still only in their early sixties.)

'Well, it seems as if the rest of the Supreme Court bench has come to see you all off,' I observed, but looking around, I realized that Philanderer and Cumquat were now nowhere in sight.

Then we couldn't find Pomfret's fishing-basket. 'Someone must have moved it,' he said. Someone in fact had, because it finally turned up on the other side of the car from where we had left it. At the time we thought nothing of this. It was only later that it assumed a more sinister aspect. Picking up the basket, and slinging the leather strap over one shoulder, Pomfret made his way down to the jetty where the yacht, with Opscotch and the three-legged dog aboard, was now moored.

As I helped the party of fishermen put their baskets and fishing gear aboard, I had the odd feeling that we were being closely observed. I looked around, but could see nobody in particular. Cumquat and Philanderer were still nowhere in sight.

Finally the fishermen were under sail, and off into the Bay. I watched them for a while as their spinnaker caught and swelled to the eager sea breeze, and then I drove home.

Meanwhile, the yacht skimmed quickly over the water to a point a mile or so offshore, where they furled their sails and dropped anchor. The water was calm, the sun was warm, no cloud in the sky.

'I might go in for a dip before we start fishing,' Pomfret suggested, and as none of the judges offered any objection, he peeled off down to his briefs and dived in. He swam about fifty metres and as he turned, he found that the three-legged dog had also jumped in and followed him.

Just at that minute he noticed Opscotch standing at the side of the yacht, beckoning him, 'We forgot to bring bait,' Opscotch called. 'Do you have any?'

'In my fishing basket,' Harry shouted back, cupping his hands. Treading water, he watched as the Judge picked up the basket, undid the straps, went to open the lid—

Then there was a tremendous explosion BOOM! which lifted the yacht clean out of the water, and sent spars and canvas and bits and pieces of boat flying in all directions . . .

A passing launch picked up Harry and the three-legged dog, but none of the three judges was ever seen again, though the Water Police and the Navy searched the bottom of the Bay for several days, with the aid of scuba divers, grappling irons, and the most modern ultra-sonic submarine devices.

I was so upset by all this that for the next six weeks I refused to eat any fish caught in the Bay, out of respect for Their Honours. *Requiescant in pace.*

LAST CARD IN THE PACK

'Did it ever occur to you,' I asked Pomfret as we returned from the Memorial Service at St Paul's Cathedral for the late Sir Anthony Opscotch, Mr Justice Peewee and Mr Justice Plump, 'that perhaps a Supreme Court judge might not be at all pleased at the prospect of a son appearing out of the blue, to embarrass him?'

Pomfret looked at me squarely: "I am determined to find out which judge is my father.'

'Perhaps your father is just as determined to make sure you do not.'

Pomfret thought for a minute. 'Do you suspect that the explosion on the yacht was deliberately planned?' he asked.

'I didn't suggest that,' I replied firmly, 'and there is no reason to jump to such a conclusion. The petrol tank for the auxiliary engine might have developed a leak. There could be a dozen explanations—'

'Including a bomb in my fishing basket? Someone did move it while we were down watching the boat being put in the water.'

'Don't let your imagination run away with you,' I countered quickly. 'All I say is that though you were the apple of your mother's eye, you may be just a grub in the apple, as far as your father is concerned.'

He fell silent, and we were overtaken by Macquarie Q.C., also returning from paying his last respects to the memory of the three defunct judges.

'Congratulations, Pomfret,' he remarked, wrily. 'That brings your score to eight, if my arithmetic is correct.'

I attempted to divert the conversation: 'Who do you think they will appoint in their place?' I asked.

'*Whom* . . .' Pomfret murmured. '*Whom* . . .'

I swallowed and began again: 'Whom do you think they will appoint in their place?'

'Not me, for one,' Macquarie stated vehemently. 'The Attorney-General sounded me out, but I told him directly that I'd rather be a quick Silk than a dead Judge. I've got a wife and family to support, you know,' he added, with a tinge of bitterness.

'I dare say the Attorney-General will soon find somebody.'

'I doubt it,' Macquarie snorted, glancing sideways at Pomfret. 'I've discussed the matter with the other Senior men at the Bar, and we are unanimous that none of us will accept an appointment to the Supreme Court until there is a full enquiry into this rash of sudden, violent deaths of so many judges. Preferably a Royal Commission.'

'The Coroner was satisfied in each case that there were no suspicious circumstances.'

'Taken alone, that might seem so, but when they are dying in series, one after the other, even two or three at a time, it sounds like more than a coincidence.'

And he stalked on ahead of us.

'I really think,' I said at last, 'that you ought to give up this search for your father.'

'No.' Pomfret's voice was determined.

'Well,' I sighed, 'there is only one possibility left – Mr Justice Cumquat. And surely nobody in his wildest dreams, not even you, would want a father like Cumquat. So why not forget about the whole thing?'

Still Pomfret was unshaken: 'Will you help me to meet Mr Justice Cumquat?'

'Anything for a quiet life,' I groaned. 'But this time we shall have to be very, very cautious.'

We were then passing the Supreme Court entrance and the judges' limousines had just pulled up to discharge their valuable judicial cargo, also returning from the Memorial Service. We paused respectfully to let Their Honours cross the footpath unimpeded, when we were confronted by Sir George Philanderer and Mr Justice Cumquat.

'Morning, Dominic,' Sir George nodded. 'A sad day.'

'A very sad day, Judge,' I assented. 'Your brother Opscotch showed me many kindnesses over the years. And your brothers

Peewee and Plump already had displayed great promise of a distinguished career on the Bench. Very sad.' Then remembering my manners, I gestured towards my companion. 'You have met my pupil, Harry Pomfret?'

Philanderer looked him over in a very unfriendly fashion. 'Humph,' he growled.

'Humph!' squeaked Cumquat, standing on tip-toe.

And as one, they about-faced and hurried towards the entrance to Judges' Chambers.

As I watched their abrupt departure, I remarked to Pomfret, 'It would appear that old Opscotch did get around to telling Cumquat that you suspected him of being your father.'

When we arrived in Chambers, there was a letter for Harry, from Clare. He opened it and immediately counted the number of pages. I can never understand why young people in love gauge their opposite number's devotion according to how long are the letters they write.

'Nine pages,' he gloated.

'They may be nine pages full of abuse, for all you know,' I badgered him, 'or a description of some other young man she has met.'

He grinned, and for the next seven minutes read and re-read Clare's letter. 'She wants to come back to Melbourne,' he said at last, looking up triumphantly, 'but she is having some trouble arranging another transfer of her training as a social worker. She says the hospitals frown on too much chopping and changing.'

'Quite so, quite so,' I nodded. I didn't say what I really thought, that it would be better all round if Clare stayed in Sydney for the full six months. I didn't want any more trouble with her father. I hoped that by the time Clare did return, Harry would have finished his period of Reading law, and would be set up in Chambers of his own, and no longer any responsibility of mine. Naturally I felt a lot of sympathy for my pupil, but after all, my friendship with cousin George went back a long way, before Harry was even born.

And while I was pondering the matter of Harry's birth—or rather, his conception—my thoughts strayed to the question of Mr Justice Cumquat.

'There is absolutely no need for you to do anything,' I told

Harry. 'Seeing that Opscotch has informed Cumquat of your suspicions, the next move is up to him. If he really is your father, he is sure to take the opportunity of speaking to you privately, the first chance he gets.'

'But I never see him privately,' Harry protested. 'In fact, today was the first time I've ever seen him close-up.'

All of which was true enough. Judges lead a cloistered life—they never go for a drink in a bar, you never sit next to one in the train, or bump into one in Myers. You may catch a glimpse of a judge in the Members' Stand at the races or at the Melbourne Cricket Ground, but as a rule, a sighting of a judge outside the Law Courts is more rare than the sighting of a yellow-bellied crested shrike-tit.

However—'He does come over to lunch in the Common Room fairly often,' I pointed out. 'If you manage things properly, you could get to sit next to him. But—' I raised my voice slightly, to emphasize the point, 'but on no account broach the topic of whether or not he is your father. Let him bring it up. You just sit there and say nothing.'

And so it was that several days later, Mr Justice Cumquat found himself eating lunch next to a young man who preserved an ominous silence throughout the entire meal. His Honour found this quite off-putting, and when the same thing happened when he came again to Barristers' Chambers for lunch later that week, the same ominous, sinister silence, and then again the next week, the Judge became very uneasy and resolved thenceforth to lunch in the solitude and security of his own Club.

But Pomfret was a young man of infinite resource. He managed to strike up an acquaintance with Cumquat's tipstaff, and was thereafter kept fully informed of where the Judge would be at any given time. A judge's tipstaff is almost *en famille*. He runs errands, makes cups of tea, eases his judge through the little inconsequential matters of everyday life, and generally knows more about what the judge will be doing, and when, and where, than even the judge's wife.

And so it happened that when Mr Justice and Mrs Cumquat were one weekend wandering through the Garden Week displays in the Exhibition Building, as His Honour bent down to smell the perfume of some rare carnation, he found Harry Pomfret also sniffing at a carnation on the next bench.

This represented something of a triumph of persistence and ingenuity on Harry's part. Victoria is rightly called the Garden State—in Melbourne not only are the public parks and avenues lush and green, but everywhere the gardens of private homes overflow with vegetation and a blaze of colour so profuse that, from a distance, all sight of the houses is lost under an overhanging mantle of trees and shrubbery. With so many enthusiastic home-gardeners, the Garden Week display is a magnet which draws Melburnians from all directions.

Because Clare was still in Sydney, Harry had borrowed Amelia Mutt from Gerard, to accompany him. As he searched through the immense crowd to find Mr Justice Cumquat, Amelia simpered 'Oh, Hawwy . . . Oh, Hawwy . . .' until his head began to spin.

But there at last, he was successful. He sniffed at his carnation, and Cumquat sniffed at the adjoining one. It was more than Cumquat could do to ignore Harry completely. He felt constrained to give a brisk nod, clear his throat with a squeaky 'Hrrmph . . . Hrrmph . . .', then seize his wife by the arm and whisk her off through the crowd to a display of compost bins and chook manure fertilisers.

'Oh, Hawwy . . .' gurgled Amelia Mutt.

That night Mr Justice and Mrs Cumquat went to the Opera. Not that Cumquat was an ardent theatre-goer. Far from it. The last occasion he had been to the theatre was to see Gladys Moncrieff in *The Maid of the Mountains*. But this time Joan Sutherland was singing *La Traviata* and his wife had insisted.

The theatre was packed. Fifteen minutes before the curtain went up there wasn't a vacant seat in the house—except for the two seats right next to the Cumquats. Just as the lights dimmed and the orchestra was about to burst into the Overture, the two late-comers arrived. With some misgiving His Honour heard them stumbling over feet as they made their way along the row, 'Excuse me, sir . . . Excuse me, lady . . .' and in the background a giggling 'Oh, Hawwy . . .'

Pomfret sat next to the Judge, and throughout the entire evening not a word was exchanged. Cumquat sat there in contained fury, his tiny rage by no means abated by finding that they were singing the opera in Italian and he couldn't understand a word of it. What with one thing and the other, he could hardly restrain himself from striking Harry.

Only when the final curtain fell did Harry speak. As he and Amelia Mutt prepared to leave, he turned to the Judge and said quite politely, 'Good evening, father.'

'What did the young man say?' Mrs Cumquat enquired.

'Nothing dear, nothing,' her spouse squealed, and pushed her off in the other direction, with the sound of 'Oh Hawwy . . . Oh Hawwy . . .' echoing in his ears.

Harry reported these events to me, with not a little disappointment.

'He hasn't given the slightest sign that he might be my father,' he complained.

'You can hardly expect him to hug you to his bosom as a long-lost son,' I replied, 'not with his wife standing there.'

So when Mr Justice Cumquat was perched in the barber's chair, three days later, whom was he startled to see, sitting in the next chair?

'Good morning, Judge,' Harry chirped.

'H'm,' Cumquat squeaked, suspiciously.

'Tried any interesting cases lately?' Harry persisted.

Trapped in his barber's chair, Cumquat felt very vulnerable. 'You knows I can't discuss cases I try in Court, Mr . . . er . . . Mr . . .'

'Pomfret, Harry Pomfret.' Then, really getting into his stride, 'I was conceived at the Pig and Whistle Hotel in the Blue Mountains on the Queen's Birthday weekend in 1956. I don't suppose you've ever been there?'

Cumquat looked quite startled. 'Well, as a matter of fact, I have.'

'You have!' Harry exclaimed in delight and excitement. Then leaning across, he whispered conspiratorially, 'So you *are* my father!'

His Honour recoiled, looked around in dismay, suddenly jumped out of the barber's chair and hurried from the shop, throwing a twenty-dollar note on the counter as he went. Only when he was half-way back to the Law Courts did he realize that he was still wearing the barber's wrap-around. Tearing it from his neck, he screwed it up into a small ball and threw it furiously into the gutter.

The following week the Supreme Court Bench suffered another set-back. Mr Justice Trot resigned. The official explanation was that he was in poor health, but in actual fact the poor old chap was scared stiff. The sudden disappearance of his brother judges, one after the other, had got to him at last, and when Sir Anthony Opscotch, Mr Justice Peewee and Mr Justice Plump were simultaneously detonated into oblivion, it was the last straw. Trot quite lost his nerve and retired to the safety of suburban life. (Unfortunately, three weeks later he was climbing a ladder to inspect his T.V. aerial when he lost his balance, fell to the ground, broke his neck, out-outed his brief candle, and flights of angels sang him to his rest. But that is another story).

No sooner had the news of Mr Justice Trot's resignation become known, than we received a visit from Macquarie.

'Nine!' he declared stonily, as he stood in the doorway of my Chambers.

It was more than I could stand. 'Why don't you go drown yourself, you great, parsimonious, puffed-up prig!' I bellowed. 'And if it's of any interest to you, as soon as my Reader has finished with the judges, he's going to start on the Q.C.'s.'

Macquarie's jaw dropped and he looked at me in amazement. Then, not knowing what to say, he turned and left. I must confess that if I had surprised Macquarie by my outburst, I had surprised myself even more. I looked at Pomfret who was gazing at me in disbelief.

'Sorry,' I grimaced in embarrassment, 'Can't stand that chap.'

Pomfret continued to gaze at me in awe until, rather nettled, I snapped, 'You are supposed to be preparing an Originating Summons for me, aren't you? Well, do it.'

And not another word passed between us during the morning. However, just before he went out to lunch, he came and stood in front of my desk, like a schoolboy.

'Well, what is it?' I growled, in a gruff voice.

'Thanks,' he smiled shyly, and left.

There was no doubt that things in the Supreme Court were becoming serious. With not enough judges to go around, the backlog of cases was piling up. Litigants were complaining bitterly at the undue delay, solicitors were at their wits' end trying to explain to their clients why their cases hadn't come on for hearing, and protesting letters to the Editor were starting to appear in the daily papers. If things go on this way much longer, I thought to myself, the whole process of the law will grind to a halt. And if we lose any more judges! I shuddered at the thought.

The Senior Bar remained adamant: None of them would accept appointment to the Supreme Court Bench until the mystery of so many dead judges was thoroughly investigated. It had by now become crystal clear that Macquarie and his merry men held Harry somehow responsible, and they would be satisfied with nothing but his scalp. By hook or by crook they would find some means to have him disbarred.

MORE WORK FOR THE UNDERTAKER

The next day I had to appear in the Court of Appeal. In our State, a judge must be a man for all seasons. One month he will spend presiding over murder trials, the next month interpreting the meaning of vaguely worded Wills, the next hearing damages cases for motor accident victims, the next deciding the effect of the small print in long and complex contracts . . . And then, from time to time, he must sit as a judge in the Court of Appeal, listening to heavy legal argument as to why and how one of his brothers judges went wrong.

The three judges I had drawn to hear my Appeal were Philanderer, Cumquat and Mr Justice Guff. There they sat in their scarlet and ermine, like the Three Wise Monkeys, waiting to shoot me down in flames. And as for seeing no evil, hearing no evil, speaking no evil, nothing could have been further from their minds.

I was briefed to appear for the manufacturers of a large metal press, an enormous machine, bigger than the size of a suburban home. Its operation was simple: a workman pressed a button and down fell a large hammer, weighing several tonnes. With a tremendous crash and with the force of an express train brought to a sudden halt, the hammer would strike a piece of warm metal and mould it into the desired shape. All very simple, but what happened between the workman pushing the button, and the hammer falling, was rather complex.

Armed with photographs, designs, plans, specifications and working drawings, I endeavoured to explain: 'You see, Y'r Honours, this thing goes in here, and that thing goes in there, and you press this, and that makes this thing move along here. Then this other thing moves up like so, and that makes that other thing move down like so, and then of course this thing here slides back towards that other thing there—'

'I don't quite follow,' Mr Justice Guff murmured. 'Perhaps if Counsel would repeat that.'

I started again: 'This little thing here is connected to that big thing there, and that big thing in turn is connected to this thing here, and this thing goes in here and that thing goes in there, and you press this, and that makes this thing move along here—'

'Which thing?' Mr Justice Cumquat squeaked.

'This thing, Y'r Honour. This thing here,' I replied.

'Oh, that thing?'

'Yes, that thing.'

'Oh . . .' and Cumquat sat back.

'But what about this thing?' Mr Justice Philanderer asked.

'What thing?'

'This thing here.'

'Oh, that thing!' I replied confidently. 'Well, Y'r Honour, that thing there moves up like so, and that makes this other thing move down like so, and this thing here slides back towards that other thing—'

'What other thing?' Cumquat squeaked, again sitting forward.

'This thing.'

'Oh . . .' and once more he retreated into his high-backed throne-like chair.

'I should be obliged,' Mr Justice Guff murmured again, 'if Counsel would start at the beginning and repeat all that.'

I gave up. 'If Y'r Honours would visit the factory and inspect the press?' I suggested.

At this the three of them went into a huddle, whispering together for about five minutes, while we all waited patiently. At length they sat back in their thrones and Philanderer intoned in sepulchral, god-like cadence, 'The Court has considered Counsel's request that we view the press, and my brother judges and I have decided to accede to that request. Would Counsel make the necessary arrangements? The Court will now adjourn.'

'All stand!' shouted the tipstaff, 'This Honourable Court stands adjourned *sine die*. God save the Queen!'

I invited Pomfret to come along with me to the View, and as we sat in the back of the taxi on the way, I explained to him what the case was all about.

The Court of Appeal

'You see,' I said, spreading out the diagrams, 'this thing goes in here, and that thing goes in there, and . . .'

When I had finished my explanation, Pomfret sat there for a quite a while, with a rather stunned look on his face. 'I see,' he said at last, 'but what if this thing goes along here instead of along there?'

'Where? What thing? Along where?' I exclaimed in alarm.

'This thing. Along there,' he repeated.

I sat gazing at the diagrams in consternation. 'If it does, my boy,' I groaned, 'I have lost the Appeal.'

The factory where the press was situated was an enormous galvanized iron shed, as large as an aircraft hangar. There were no windows, only large doors, and in the gloom we could see dirt and grease covering everything. In the middle of the factory stood the press. One of the workmen operated it for us, pressing the button, and down fell the great hammer with a deafening roar, making the whole building shake and rattle. Not surprisingly, all the workmen were deaf, and we had to shout and wave our arms in the air to make them understand.

Cumquat and Philanderer went to inspect the switchboard, where the button was. Mr Justice Guff went off to have a look at the platform to which the hammer fell, and Harry went with him to hold his papers. I stood respectfully back, with m' learned friend, so as not to overhear what the Judges might say to one another. As we waited there, I happened to glance over to see what Mr Justice Guff was doing and was startled to see that he and Harry had walked on to the platform, right under where the hammer fell.

'Pomfret!' I shouted, 'Get out of there!'

He looked towards me. 'What?' he called.

'Get out of there!' I shouted again.

He still could not hear, and took several steps towards me. At which very moment the hammer suddenly started to move, dropping straight down, down, with incredible speed. There was a resounding crash like the roar of thunder, the whole building shook, and the hammer began slowly to rise again. It had missed Harry by no more than a cat's whisker, and then only thanks to the fact that he had walked towards me. But Mr Justice Guff!

His Honour was reduced to a wafer, the size of a large dinner plate and the thickness of a postage stamp.

I ran to the switchboard. Philanderer and Cumquat were wandering away from the Board, in different directions, both looking very, very innocent.

'Who pressed that button?' I demanded angrily.

'Button? What button?' they both asked.

'That button there,' I shouted, pointing.

'Not me,' Philanderer replied. 'Did you press that button, Cumquat?'

'Certainly not,' he squeaked, 'Never touched it.'

'One of you must have touched it, otherwise the hammer wouldn't have fallen.'

Then Philanderer turned very nasty. 'That's what you say, Dominic. That's what this case is all about. But seeing is believing. I didn't press the button. Mr Justice Cumquat didn't press the button. Therefore the machine does malfunction, as the plaintiff alleged. I'm afraid you've lost your Appeal.' He smiled sourly.

'Someone had better phone an ambulance,' Cumquat remarked.

'On no, Y'r Honour,' I snarled. 'It's an undertaker we need. And he'd better bring a trowel to scrape up the remains.'

Words of this tragedy had already reached Chambers even before we arrived back. The first person we saw when we entered the foyer was Macquarie Q.C. I have no doubt he was waiting there for us.

'Ten!' he sniffed.

Pomfret and I passed him without a word. We were both quite shaken by what had happened, and it took us several days before we could get the ringing noise of that hammer out of our ears.

'I wonder what made the hammer drop like that?' Pomfret remarked.

'The machine malfunctioned,' I answered shortly, and refused to discuss the matter any further.

Next afternoon the late-delivery mail brought two letters for Harry. One was from Clare and he opened it eagerly and read. 'She will arrive back in Melbourne the day after next,' he announced gloatingly, for he had hardly forgiven me for persuading her to go away. Then he opened the second letter and frowned. He read it several times, before handing it to me. The note was typewritten:

DEAR HARRY,

I MUST SEE YOU. I SHALL BE IN THE TREASURY GARDENS AT THE PRESIDENT KENNEDY MEMORIAL AT 7 P.M. SHARP THIS EVENING. PLEASE COME ALONE.

WITH WARM REGARDS,
YOUR FATHER.

I looked at Pomfret. 'Do you intend to go?' I asked.

'Certainly,' he replied.

'I don't like it,' I commented. 'Not after that accident the other day.'

'But you said that was a malfunction of the machine.'

'I'm not so sure,' I replied. 'What with Sir Anthony Opscotch's yacht blowing up, and then that hammer inexplicably falling, I'm beginning to suspect that your life may be in danger.'

'But I've got to go,' Harry persisted. 'It may be my only chance to find out who is my father.'

'Well, be careful,' I warned him.

It was already dark and I was still working late in Chambers when he left. 'Good luck,' I called after him.

* * * * *

When Harry arrived at the President Kennedy Memorial, it was quite dark and desolate. The park lights nearest the Memorial were out—probably broken by vandals, he thought. He tried to check the time on his watch, but could not properly see where the hands were pointing. As he squinted, he heard a sudden slight sound behind him, but before he could turn, he was struck heavily on the back of the head and lost consciousness.

ALL ABOARD FOR SAUDI ARABIA

That night I could hardly sleep and kept tossing and turning, going over and over in my mind the extraordinary sequence of events which had followed one another in rapid succession since Harry Pomfret first became my pupil.

He had come to me on Gerard's recommendation, so Arthur said. I sincerely wished Gerard had minded his own business and applied his energies to becoming a competent doctor, instead of always running around chasing this female and that female. If only he'd marry some sensible girl and settle down. Or marry any girl, sensible or not, and settle down. Even Amelia Mutt would do.

I rolled over and tugged the blankets up about my ears.

On reflection however, perhaps not. Any girl—except Amelia Mutt! The prospect of tiny tots trailing around after me bleating, 'Oh Gwandpa . . . Oh Gwandpa . . .' made my blood run cold.

I rolled over again and re-arranged the blankets.

Pomfret's father was a Supreme Court judge, so it had to be either Cumquat or George Philanderer. But George had given me his word that Harry was not his son, and I couldn't believe George would lie to me. From our Terrible Twins days at the University I knew that he was reckless, completely unscrupulous if necessary, but he wouldn't tell a lie about an important matter like that.

I punched my pillow into a more comfortable shape.

Still, George was Jesuit educated—he was trained in logic, to pick and choose his words carefully. What had been his exact words? . . . Perhaps he had told me the literal truth, but in such a way as to mislead me, to give me a false impression, to make me jump to the wrong conclusion. Didn't the Jesuits say that the end justifies the means?

I punched again at my pillow, rather savagely.

No, it was probably Machiavelli who said that . . . Still, six of one and half a dozen of the other. The Jesuits are very deep, quite inscrutable. There are only three things that God doesn't know: how many Nuns there are in the world; how much money the Franciscans have got; and what the Jesuits will do next!

I sat up in bed and switched on the bedside lamp.

Thank God for the Christian Brothers . . . Nothing intellectual about them. All they gave us was the strap, multiple football injuries, and an abiding guilt complex.

The light of the bedside lamp woke Amy. 'Can't you sleep, dear?' she asked.

'I was a bit restless.'

'I'm not surprised. Only last night I read in the paper that your Stars are in turmoil in the Zodiac. No wonder you woke up.' She started to get out of bed.

'Where are you going?' I asked.

'To make you a snack, to help you get back to sleep. We must keep your strength up, mustn't we, so you will win your cases.' She shuffled her feet into her slippers. 'You know, Dominic, I think the solicitors send you all their difficult briefs on purpose.' She sighed. 'But then, if it's in your Stars, there's nothing you can do about it. You can't win a trial if the constellations are against you, can you?'

She bustled off to the kitchen to make me a snack, bless her. So then, not only couldn't I sleep, but I also had indigestion!

When Harry didn't arrive in Chambers that morning and when there was no word from him the whole day, I began to be alarmed. It occurred to me that I was possibly the only person in Melbourne who would have particularly noticed his absence. Should I inform the Missing Persons Bureau? Not knowing what to do, I did nothing, but as I made my way back home to *Chez Amy* I found that I was a bundle of nerves.

Meanwhile, when he recovered consciousness, Harry had found himself in total darkness. Moving a little, he bumped into a wall and, groping, followed it around until he realized that he was imprisoned in a room—a room without doors. He wondered how he had got there. Stretching up, and standing on tip-toe, he could not reach the ceiling, and he discovered that there was no furniture, no window, nothing but four walls. The

Must keep your strength up

walls were of metal, corrugated, and he suspected that he was in some sort of galvanized iron shed, and that someone must have lowered him in there through the roof.

He stumbled over something on the floor. Kneeling, he found that whoever had put him there had also provided him with a cut-lunch of corned beef and cucumber sandwiches, and a vacuum flask of hot coffee.

He listened. Outside he could hear a sort of shuffling sound and the occasional bleat of some animals. He listened more carefully. The bleats that he could hear were familiar . . . Sheep baaing! So he was in the country. The baas seemed to come from near and far, as if from an enormous flock of sheep.

Then he heard voices, voices chanting, chanting all together, voices in a foreign language. They reminded him of a television documentary he had once seen of a multitude of Moslems prone on their prayer mats, all facing Mecca and reciting the Koran.

He became unpleasantly aware of some sort of instability of his prison. It seemed to move, it seemed to rock, this way, that way, gently to and fro. The room was firm, but it was unsteady. The motion was regular, but uneven. It made him feel a bit dizzy.

Then he understood! He was on a ship.

What he did not know was that he was in a container on the top deck of a merchant vessel carrying exports of live sheep to the Middle East. Harry Pomfret was on his way to Saudi Arabia!

But those whom the gods love . . .

While still in Australian waters, the Islam equivalent of a Second-Mate fell ill, and the ship's cook-cum-doctor diagnosed appendicitis. The Captain and officers held a hurried conference and, having discarded their original intention of throwing the Second-Mate overboard, they decided to put into the nearest port and seek medical aid. So they turned to starboard and set sail for Fremantle, where they berthed in late afternoon.

The arrival of a ship full of sheep aroused the curiosity of the stevedores on the wharf, but even more interest was excited by the sight of a solitary container sitting all alone on the top deck, in the middle of a mob of Merinos.

'They've probably got something pretty valuable in there,' one wharfie remarked to another, who repeated this to a third, who repeated it to a fourth. By the time the story had gone the rounds,

Wharf 8 of the Fremantle docks was abuzz with the rumour that 'that there container' was full of gold and jewels, a veritable Arabian Nights treasure.

Night fell. Under cover of darkness, one of the great cranes on the wharf slowly nudged its way, high in the air, over the ship. A dogman was lowered gently towards the deck, steel hawsers were attached to the container—and Harry was airborne.

The boom of the crane slewed slowly sideways, cautiously descended, placing the container on the back of a waiting truck, and Harry was again in transit.

An hour later, in the deserted wilderness of scrub, and amid muted exclamations of great excitement, the top of the container was skilfully detached. When the wharfies saw their loot, they were astonished. Quite disappointed, in fact.

'What are you doing there?' they called down to Harry.

'I've been kidnapped,' he explained.

So they convened an impromptu union meeting among themselves.

'He must be valuable, or they wouldn't have put him there,' one of the wharfies observed.

'Why don't we hold him to ransom?' another suggested, 'that way we'd get enough to pay for expenses and something else extra all round.'

'But we don't know who put him there,' one wharfie objected.

So they went back to lean over the edge of the container, to parley with Harry. But when he told them that he was an orphan, all alone in the world, they were reduced to tears and took around the hat for him. So generous in their giving were those great soft-hearted men that when Harry counted the proceeds, he found that he not only had enough to pay for his plane fare, first-class, back to Melbourne, but also sufficient to buy several post-cards of black swans, a dried flower arrangement of West Australian wildflowers for Clare, and a small bottle of Swan Lager to drink while he waited for the plane to depart.

The wharfies came to see him off, and as his plane left the tarmac he looked down at them standing there on the Observation Deck, tears in their eyes, waving their pocket handkerchieves as he disappeared up, up and into the wide blue yonder.

Back in Melbourne, despairing of ever seeing Harry Pomfret

again, I had told Arthur to return any briefs on his desk to the solicitors who had sent them, with apologies and explanation that Mr Pomfret was indisposed.

So of course when Pomfret, newly arrived from Perth, suddenly walked into my Chambers, my anxiety immediately gave way to irritation.

'Nice of you to call in,' I remarked icily. 'I had thought you understood that a pupil is not allowed to be absent from Chambers without his Master's permission.'

'I was kidnapped,' Harry gasped.

'Nonsense!' I retorted, without thinking. Then, as what he had said sunk in, I asked, 'You were what?'

'Kidnapped,' he repeated and briefly told me his story.

'I can't stay and talk at the moment,' I said at length. 'I have to make an appearance in the Court of Appeal.' Then recollecting that both Cumquat and Philanderer were still hearing Appeals, I added, 'You'd better come too. Just sit behind me in Court.'

The Banco Court, in which the Judges of Appeal sit, has the same high, high ceiling, the same elaborate decor as the other courts, but its architecture is much more intimate. It is almost a Court in the round, so that it is virtually impossible for anybody to enter the well of the Court without attracting the attention of the three judges.

As I pushed open the half-glass panel doors, with Pomfret at my heels like a faithful spaniel, I kept my eyes on the judges—or rather, on Philanderer and Cumquat. Without letting their attention stray from the arguments of Counsel addressing them, they glanced idly at me as I entered, at Pomfret, just as idly watched us as we sat down, and then gazed blankly once more at the rattled Silk who was trying in vain to convince them that black was white, or even, as a desperate last resort, grey.

If I had expected one of the two judges to show some surprise at the sight of Harry, I was disappointed. Their apparent disinterest could not have been more complete.

But as we later returned to Chambers, it was Macquarie Q.C. who showed surprise. He stopped stock-still in his tracks and gasped to Pomfret, 'I thought you were gone for good.'

'Really?' I murmured smoothly, 'and what made you think so?'

For a moment Macquarie said nothing. Then, with a shake

of his head, he turned to me, 'I heard that your clerk had returned all his briefs to the instructing solicitors.'

'Pomfret can't do every case solicitors want him for,' I smiled sweetly. 'He can't be in four different courts at once, you know.'

'But,' stammered Macquarie, 'But—'

'Never mind, old chap,' I went on. 'Next time my pupil has to return a brief because he's so busy, I'll make sure you get first offer of it.' And on we sailed.

When we arrived in my Chambers, Pomfret was about to resume his labours, to pick up where he had left off.

But at that very moment Arthur entered my Chambers. 'This brief has just been delivered for Mr Pomfret,' he announced.

'What sort of a case is it, Arthur?' I enquired.

'Civil Juries. My, we are coming on, aren't we? A Supreme Court brief for the plaintiff in a jury trial! Congratulations, Mr Pomfret.' Then, looking anxiously at me, he asked, 'Do you think he can manage it?'

'He can try,' I reassured him. 'What's the plaintiff's name?'

'Tubb,' Arthur replied, 'Joseph Tubb.'

'And which judge?'

'Mr Justice Cumquat,' Arthur smiled. 'His Honour will keep Mr Pomfret on his toes, I should think.'

'If he lives,' I sighed as I shrugged off my gown, perched my wig on Voltaire's bald pate, and began to unfasten my wing collar.

DR HU'S CHINESE PUZZLE

Joe Tubb was a very ordinary Australian. His schooldays had been a running battle with the teachers, punctuated by regular visits from the truant inspector. When he had at last emerged from his bleak educational chrysalis into the bright world of warm sunshine and colour and had spread his new-found wings, he discovered that he had not turned into a beautiful butterfly, but into a rather drab moth. Not for him the gaudy flight from one dazzling flower bed to another, but a covert flutter around the vegetable patch.

At the age of 28 years he found himself drearily chained to an already tired wife, and the very indifferent father of five grubby children of assorted shapes and sizes, always with sores and always with runny noses. He never kept a job for long, and each employment was a little less salubrious than the last. Life had given him nothing, and held nothing in store for him.

Or so it seemed.

He was a member of a gang of workmen, contracted to repair the asphalt footpaths at the Zoo. Joe's job was to tidy up any breaks in the pavement, wait until a blob of asphalt was poured into each hole, smooth down the hot asphalt, then spread sand and fine gravel over. He worked steadily, thinking of what horse would win at the races on Saturday, who would be chosen to play for the football team he followed . . . To his surroundings he paid little heed. He passed the ostriches and flamingoes without a glance. The black panther and the leopards tried to attract his attention in vain. The lions roared, the hyenas laughed, the elephants trumpeted and the humming birds hummed, but Joe Tubb had eyes for nothing but holes in the asphalt footpath.

Still intent, he came at last to the simian enclosures. There were few visitors to the Zoo that day, and man's nearest relations were a little bit bored. There was practically nobody for them to stare at. The spider monkeys chattered encouragingly at Joe, but he ignored them. The baboons ran around their rocks, and the orang-outangs swung from one trapeze to another, expecting some sort of applause, some recognition. But Joe was too busy with his shovel and pick. They tried again, with excited grunts and coughs. In vain. It was, as they say in the theatre, a dead audience.

The gorillas were amazed. Nobody, just nobody, ever passed them without stopping, and gawking, and gaping. They were quite affronted by Joe's insensitivity, and whispered rude remarks about him in each other's ear. Old King Kong, who had been more than 15 years in the business, had never seen anything like it. In some irritation he stood up and with his great fists began to beat his chest, the way Tarzan had taught him. Joe Tubb did not even lift his head. In utter and complete exasperation, King Kong picked up a handful of bananas, threw them somewhat awkwardly and somewhat aimlessly, and scored a direct hit.

It was at this very moment that Joe's Leading-hand came up around the corner of the path, just in time to witness King Kong throw the bunch of bananas which hit Joe on the head. Surprised, Joe sat down plomp on the footpath, then looked about him, half-dazed, wondering what had happened. The Leading-hand called some of the other workmen and they formed a semi-circle around Joe, keeping all the time a careful eye on the gorilla who, now satisfied that he had acquired an attentive audience, was making an elaborate display of searching for fleas on his favourite wife.

'What should we do?' The Leading-hand asked.

'Joe will have to go the doctor,' one of the workmen replied. 'He might be badly injured.'

This workman was the Union rep on the job, and he helped stand Joe up. The rep then gave Joe the address of a proper doctor—one who knows all about these things, he told him, with a meaning wink. So off Joe went to consult Dr Hu.

Dr Hu was a promising young medico of Oriental descent and his consulting rooms were on the first floor, directly above a Chinese Restaurant. Not for his patients the antiseptic smell of anaesthetics and sodium dichlorate: Dr Hu's consulting rooms were forever pervaded by the delicious aroma of chicken chow mein and crisp skin duck.

Despite his Asian antecedents, Dr Hu had a taste for English tailors, Italian shoes, French silk ties, Swiss watches, Swedish cars and Scotch whisky. He had a Polish wife, an Armenian girl friend, a German shepherd dog, a Filipino housemaid and medical degrees from New Zealand and Alabama. His tastes were expensive and might have been difficult to appease, had he not made an important discovery quite early in his career. Not for him the painstaking burning of the midnight oil to discover penicillin or the techniques of anterior spinal fusion. No, he had achieved universal esteem and prestige by the simple device of marching. Protest marching. He joined marches to protest against whaling, against killing baby seals, against building dams, against nuclear war, against shooting kangaroos. He carried banners and joined marches in favour of euthenasia, conservation, women's lib, gay lib, prisoners' rights, civil rights, abortion, in vitro fertilization, wildlife protection, universal disarmament—Wherever two or three were gathered together, there was Dr Hu, remarkable in his heavy horn-rimmed spectacles and Saville Row suits.

Consequently his professional fame spread far and wide. The trendies reassured one another that he was a brilliant medical man, and everyone 'left of centre' recommended him to all their friends and relations. He was the darling of the unions, the delight of the socially discontented, and well on his way to becoming a millionaire. His waiting room was forever thronged, and his consultations were perforce brief and business-like, with no time for banal chit-chat and bedside manner.

'Well, and what's wrong with you?' he asked Joe Tubb.

'I got hurt at work,' Joe replied. 'The Union rep sent me.'

'H'm,' commented Dr Hu, and carefully noted that fact down on a card. 'Just touch your toes.'

Joe did as directed, and then lifted his shirt while Dr Hu listened at the other end of a stethoscope.

'You've got a very sore back and you won't be fit enough to work for a fortnight,' the good doctor at length remarked, with a genuinely inscrutable Oriental smile. 'I'll give you a certificate for your employer. I'll also prescribe a spinal brace and arrange for a course of physiotherapy.'

As Joe, somewhat taken aback, was about to depart, Dr Hu pressed into his hand a business card: 'You had better go to these solicitors. They'll arrange everything for you.'

So, half an hour later, there was Joe sitting in the waiting room of Messrs Dogsbody, Doomsday and Drift, solicitors and notaries public. Of course the original partners were now dead, and in their place were the new generation – Mr Pop, Mr Snackle and Mr Crapp, all very super-efficient, with memory-bank typewriters, data processing print-outs, and time-efficiency programmes.

Joe was received into Mr Pop's office like a long-lost brother. Mr Pop perused Dr Hu's medical certificate, while his partners hung over the back of his chair, reading it at the same time.

'You're entitled to Workers' Comp,' Mr Pop promised.

'And make-up pay,' suggested Mr Snackle.

'And a common law action for damages,' esctatically cooed Mr Crapp.

'Damages for pain,' opined Mr Pop.

'Damages for suffering,' sighed Mr Snackle.

'Damages for loss of enjoyment of life,' ecstatically crooned Mr Crapp.

'We'll issue a Writ against King Kong and the Zoo,' Mr Pop panted.

'We'll sue them for negligence,' shrieked Mr Snackle.

'We'll make their insurance companies pay!' ecstatically cried Mr Crapp.

Upon which all three of them kissed one another.

Joe Tubb was not quite sure how being hit on the head by half a dozen bananas could have given him a bad back, but for the next fortnight he had a wonderful time. He mowed the back lawn and painted the front bedroom, he went to the mid-week races and watched the mid-day movies. Every second day he went to a lady physiotherapist who gently patted his prominences and pounded his pelvis, which Joe found quite exciting, albeit pointless. And the nice thing about all this was that it cost him nothing, not a penny, and what's more he was still being paid his wages without having to do any work.

So when he reported back to Dr Hu after a pleasant fortnight's holiday, he sadly confessed that he was no better. In fact, he complained, he was much worse.

'Then we can't send you back to work yet,' Dr Hu decided, 'I'll give you a certificate for another month off.'

Messrs Pop, Snackle and Crapp were delighted. 'We'll need a specialist's opinion to back up Dr Hu,' they carolled in chorus, and sent Joe off to a Collins Street specialist.

And that was when Joe's troubles started. The specialist wrote to the solicitors, informing them that he could find nothing wrong with their client. Pop, Snackle and Crapp tsk-tsked in annoyance, crossed the name of that doctor off their list forever, and sent Joe on a pilgrimage across the length and breadth of Melbourne. He was examined by general surgeons, orthopaedic surgeons, neurosurgeons, vascular surgeons, even, in a desperate moment, by a veterinary surgeon. He was given X-rays, discograms, tomograms, myelograms, electrocardiograms, C.T. scans, electroencephelograms, until he was more radioactive than Hiroshima. He was studied by neurologists, urologists, gynaecologists, psychiatrists, plastic surgeons, paediatricians and a faith healer. But, apart from Dr Hu, the universal medical opinion of Melbourne was that there was absolutely nothing wrong with Joe Tubb.

In the meantime, the insurance companies had been busy. They had dug up two shady-looking characters who were ready to swear that they were at the Zoo when Joe was injured, that they had seen everything that happened, and that in fact Joe had thrown the bananas at himself. Special investigators had been directed to follow Joe and, concealed in the back of a panel van or hidden in the branches of trees, they had taken thousands of feet of 16 mm film of Joe, digging in his back yard, climbing all over his roof, kicking a football with the kids, running for a train, and even lifting a railway sleeper which the investigators had thoughtfully dumped on his front lawn in the middle of the night. In short, the insurance companies had armed themselves with enough evidence to sink a ship. And they had retained Macquarie Q.C. to appear on their behalf.

Pomfret gave me the papers in his brief to look through. 'What shall I do?' he asked.

I read the brief in growing consternation. The case was hopeless. It would need divine intervention for Joe Tubb to win his action . . . A thought struck me, and I rummaged through one of the drawers of my desk.

'Here,' I said at last, handing Pomfret a small brass medallion, 'pin this inside your Bar jacket.'

'What is it?' he enquired.

'St. Jude!' I replied, triumphantly. 'The Hope of the Hopeless! The patron saint of desperate causes! Rub the medal every time the case seems to be going against you.'

'I imagine I'll be rubbing if from go to whoa,' Pomfret replied, despondently.

'Well, do so,' I encouraged him, spreading my arms out wide, 'for I assure you that there is no other way you are likely to win this case.'

Young Pomfret may not have been looking forward to this trial, but there is no doubt that the Honourable Mr Justice Cumquat was. He spent the night before the trial carefully sifting through all the documents on the Court file, and came to the unshakeable conclusion that the plaintiff was a malingerer and a fraud. Well, Joseph Tubb had picked the wrong judge for that little game. Cumquat would soon show him!

But now His Honour was having a bath. And playing with a rubber duck. He suspected that his brother judges would have frowned on such frivolity, but all his life he had played with a rubber duck in the bath, ever since he was a little boy. He splashed his bath water, as he performed feats of mental arithmetic, calculating the number of years to go before a knighthood would be bestowed on him too.

Mr Justice Cumquat was, by common consent, a good lawyer, which meant that he could remember the names of decided cases, and he never did anything not founded on precedent. But he lacked a kindness of heart. He administered the law to the chapter and verse, but Justice, that blindfolded wench, never groped her way into his Court.

Not of course that he was all steel. Indeed he could always be relied on to perform an act of charity when the barrister son of one of his intimate friends appeared in a case before him. Then the learned Judge would lean over backwards, forwards, sideways and all ways to ensure the success of the cause of such a worthy scion, irrespective of the merits of the case.

Later, when he met his friend in that very exclusive, exclusive club of which they were both members, he would remark, 'Had your boy in a case in front of me the other day. Helped him along a bit.'

And the friend would reply, 'Jolly good, Cumquat. You and your wife must come over to dinner.'

His Honour pushed his rubber duck zoom along to the end of the bath and fished it back with his toes.

The thought of his wife displeased him. She was a sour woman, and theirs was a loveless marriage. He had spawned two equally sour children, but his moments of passion had been rare and restrained. What he could never forgive his wife was that she was two inches taller than he was.

Cumquat's doctor told him he should relax, not get too excited. 'It's no good for your heart,' his doctor said. 'We're not as young as we were, are we?' and he prescribed some little red tablets which Cumquat gobbled up greedily. But the Judge did not relax, did not curb his vexation with the world, remained consumed with bitter envy of those more fortunate mortals taller than five feet nothing.

The man in the street he despised. The working classes he detested. And above all he hated plaintiffs with bad backs! Here then was a judge hardly likely to be sympathetic to poor old Joe Tubb. Here was a judge hardly likely to be sympathetic to anyone.

But now His Honour was an island, and his little rubber duck was swimming around and around him.

His mind returned to the trial over which he would preside tomorrow, and the hours he would have to waste listening to a lying malingerer perjure himself in the witness box. He expected that the plaintiff's solicitors would have briefed some incompetent junior barrister, almost newly called to the Bar, who would try to ask leading questions, who would imagine he could ignore the rules of evidence, who would understand nothing about the onus of proof.

Oh, Mr Justice Cumquat could see it all happening, as he had so often seen it happen before. Counsel would call as a witness one of the plaintiff's workmates, probably a Leading-hand, who would assure the Court that yes, he had seen the accident happen, with his own eyes: he had just turned a corner in the path at the very precise moment the gorilla had thrown

His Honour was having a bath

the bunch of bananas. Huh! Then some incompetent G.P. would get into the witness box and try to pull the wool over the jury's eyes by assuring them that the plaintiff was suffering from ligamentous and muscular damage to the low back, invisible on X-ray, but, he would assure them, crippling and disabling all the same. No doubt the plaintiff's solicitors would have dragged the plaintiff up and down the length and breadth of Collins Street unsuccessfully trying to get some sleazy specialist to say the same.

Well, Cumquat would show them. He was just the judge to put down this lying, malingering plaintiff and send him away with a flea in his ear. And he made this firm resolve, before he had even set eyes on Joe Tubb.

But, for the moment, His Honour was resolutely holding his little rubber duck underwater, wondering how long it would take it to drown.

Meanwhile, in a bastion of private enterprise in a back street of St.Kilda, Maisie informed the rest of the staff that she was knocking off work now, that she was going to finish early, because tomorrow she had to present herself at the Supreme Court for jury service. Her fellow-workers fell about in hysterics.

The front of the establishment where Maisie was employed bore a garish hand-painted sign announcing to all concerned that this dilapidated edifice was a MASAGE PARLER. Maisie had made the sign herself and her illiteracy had not deterred customers. The staff comprised three buxom broads, none of whom knew anything about massage, but all of whom knew a great deal about life. Maisie herself, with hair bleached yellow blonde, was the establishment's star attraction, especially to the dark, swarthy gentlemen from the Mediterranean countries. She was, as they say, good value.

Maisie led a double life. Night after night, for most of the year, she was a hard-working working-girl. But during school holidays she temporarily retired and became a model Mum. Then her son would come home from boarding school and Maisie would potter around their flat in a faded shapeless dress, sewing buttons on his clothes, mending any split seams, taking him to the stores to buy new socks and underwear, going with him to the pictures, spoiling him as best she could.

'You ought to get a job, Mum,' he would say, 'instead of staying cooped up at home.'

'Why should I?' she would laugh, 'we've got enough to get by, and to pay the school fees. I like being at home.'

Of course, there were some heavy overhead expenses in her business. The rent of the old building where she worked was astronomical: Still, it was owned by the Church, so at least the money went to a worthy cause. Then there were the Police—they expected a handsome pay-off. She had only reneged once, and then they had immediately swooped on the massage parlor and arrested her and the rest of the girls and charged them as common prostitutes. That had taught Maisie a lesson. She had beaten the rap, thanks to that clever young barrister Mr . . .? Mr . . .? Mr Pomfret! but from then on she always had the money ready for the Police when they called.

THE JUDGE AND THE WORKING-GIRL

The next morning Joe Tubb sat in that vast, imposing panelled courtroom, quite oppressed by the atmosphere of wigs and gowns, by the bowing and archaic formalities. He really didn't know why he was there, or how being hit on the head by half a dozen bananas thrown by a gorilla was supposed to have given him a bad back. But Dr Hu said so, and he was a doctor. And Messrs Pop, Snackle and Crapp said so, and they were solicitors, so they should know. But it was all beyond Joe Tubb's comprehension.

He heard, as in a trance, talk which he did not understand, and found refuge in keeping his steady gaze rivetted to the floor. He did not look up, even when the jurors, comprising five men and one woman, were empanelled and took the oath to try the issues in this cause, whatever that meant.

Harry Pomfret looked curiously at the one woman juror. He vaguely thought he had seen her somewhere before, but then decided he must be mistaken. Indeed Maisie in her suburban housewife gear was a different looking person from the slatternly looking tart he had once so successfully defended, and his failure to recognize her was understandable. But Maisie was under no such misapprehension. Not even Harry's wig and gown could disguise from her that he was the same smart young barrister who had got her off those charges in the Magistrates Court, and sent the Police away with a flea in their ear. This trial, Maisie thought to herself, was going to be very interesting.

Mr Justice Cumquat glared down at Joe Tubb, whose gaze was still rivetted to the floor in enormous embarrassment, and felt pitiless. The fellow was obviously putting on a show, making himself appear the picture of misery. A typical malingerer.

Then Cumquat looked speculatively and triumphantly at Pomfret in his pristine white wig. Just what the Judge had expected—this fledgling at the Bar, no doubt hopelessly incompetent, self-opinionated, and helpless at the mercy of the Bench.

'The Pleadings are not in order,' Cumquat snarled in his high-pitched squeak, 'What is the reason for that?'

'I don't know, Y'r Honour,' stammered Harry, completely taken by surprise.

'Why don't you know?' screamed Cumquat, like a mother of ten driven to distraction by some naughty five-year-old. 'You had better find out!' He sat there, quivering with indignation, secure in the knowledge that the jury were being impressed by the fact that here in living flesh was the great, the all-powerful, the omnipotent Judge.

The jury, for their part, listened in amazement, with no idea in the world what the Pleadings were, or what the fuss was all about, or why the Judge should have worked himself up into a state of near apoplexy. It was all very interesting.

But at length the trial did finally get under way. First Pomfret tried to explain to the Court, and to the jury in particular, what the case was all about, but Cumquat took the opportunity to interrupt him and to harry him incessantly, so that Pomfret's Opening Address was reduced to a bumbling and inept shambles. So far, thought His Honour, so good.

Then the plaintiff was called to take the stand. As best he could, Joe Tubb mechanically answered the questions put to him by Pomfret. But it did not take long for poor Joe to become completely bamboozled by the frequent interruptions of Cumquat, who interposed a Parthian shot whenever it seemed to him that the plaintiff's case was going too smoothly.

'On what part of your body did you fall, after you were hit by these bananas?' Cumquat squeaked.

'Er . . . er . . .' mumbled Joe.

'Speak up!' snapped His Honour in a shrill falsetto, 'I can't hear you.'

'Er . . . er . . .'

'Can't you remember?' trilled Cumquat with an unconcealed sneer.

'Yes . . . I fell backwards,' Joe explained.

'But on what part of your body did you fall?' squealed the Judge.

'Er . . .'

'Yes?'

There was a long silence, as Joe racked his simple brains trying to think of some polite reply. But try as he would, the correct answer eluded him.

'Well?' squeaked Cumquat ominously, like a cat with a mouse.

Again a long silence.

'Answer the question!' shrieked Cumquat, hitting high C, 'And speak up so we can hear you.'

Joe Tubb took a deep breath. 'I FELL ON ME ARSE!' he shouted, so loudly that everyone jumped.

Then there was a sudden hush, and one of the jurymen burst out laughing. Cumquat glanced sideways at the jury. The suburban housewife wouldn't like that sort of talk, he thought to himself with a glow of satisfaction, she wouldn't like that at all.

Macquarie Q.C., seeing which way the wind was blowing, joined forces with the Judge to give Harry a hard time, and between the two of them they were succeeding very admirably. Then Macquarie took objection to a question Harry had asked the witness, so the jury were locked up in the jury-room while legal argument as to the admissibility of the evidence was heard.

'Did you see the Judge's face when the plaintiff said that?' the Foreman laughed.

'The plaintiff's putting it on,' said another, 'there's nothing wrong with him.'

'He's a malingerer,' said a third.

The fourth and fifth agreed.

Maisie said nothing, but when they were recalled into Court, she sat herself between the Foreman and another juryman, and appeared to be listening intently to the evidence. But she wasn't. Maisie had other fish to fry.

Joe's Leading-hand took the witness stand. He had never been in a court before, but he was not concerned: he was only there to tell the truth, the whole truth and nothing but the truth. That's what he thought! . . . By the time Cumquat had finished with him, the dazed Leading-hand was agreeing that he had not seen the accident at all, in fact he had not been at work that day, he had taken a sickie. And what was more, Joe Tubb was a completely worthless individual, he was bone lazy, he was a nuisance, he caused trouble, he had no aptitude for work. When the Leading-hand at last stumbled out of the witness box, he hardly knew which way was up, and had trouble finding the door to leave the Court. Cumquat smiled amiably as the door closed behind him.

However, while all this was going on, the Foreman of the jury became aware that his leg was being gently stroked by the leg of the woman juror sitting next to him, and the stroking became more regular and more insistent. His face assumed a gentle shade of pink, which gradually deepened to a crimson blush.

Oddly enough, the face of the juror on the other side of Maisie also underwent a similar change of complexion.

The procession of witnesses rolled on. Dr Hu blinked through his large horn-rimmed spectacles in dismay when he found himself subjected to a fierce savaging by the presiding Trial Judge. Cumquat was in really good form as he tore Dr Hu apart, belittled him, mocked him, ridiculed him, made his evidence seem worthless.

When it came time for Dr Hu to be cross-examined, Macquarie Q.C. stood up, bowed to the Bench, and murmured, 'No questions, Y'r Honour.' There was no need: The Judge had already done all the work for him. If the plaintiff succeeded in this action, it would not be Cumquat's fault.

Then the jury were again locked up in their jury-room while further legal argument was heard on some abstruse point of law. When they returned to the Court, Maisie now placed herself between two other jurymen who also, in due course, displayed a heightened colour, and had great difficulty in paying attention to the evidence.

At last it was Macquarie's turn to call evidence for the Defence.

The two seedy-looking characters who claimed they had seen the accident were so unbelievable that it took all the combined resources of Macquarie and Cumquat to keep them afloat. And when Harry tried to cross-examine them, His Honour pulled out all stops, butting in, snorting, scolding, completely frustrating Harry's attempts to discredit them.

When the second of these two witnesses was about to leave the witness box, Cumquat detained him for a moment, to thank him profusely for his presence in Court and for the information which he had provided. 'No doubt what you have had to say will greatly assist the jury in their deliberations on the facts of this case,' His Honour squeaked, and cast an encouraging smirk towards the jury box.

Then he looked again at the jury . . . There seemed to be something odd about them, as if they were not listening, as if their minds were somewhere else. Cumquat began to feel uneasy. He would have been even more uneasy if he had overheard their conversation after the Court had adjourned until 10.30 o'clock the next morning.

As the jurors were leaving the precincts, Maisie said to them, 'Would you boys like to come over to my place for a drink?'

The response was unanimous, immediate, and enthusiastic.

That night, as he prepared his closing address to the jury, Harry rubbed my St. Jude medal so often and so desperately that it was burnished to a bright gleam, and almost worn through to the lead compound base underneath the bronze finish.

At the same time Cumquat was preparing his Charge to the jury, alternately swallowing little red tablets for his heart condition, and sucking a lemon.

10.30 a.m.

'All-persons-having-business-before-this-Honourable-Court-are-commanded-to-give-their-attendance-and-they-shall-be-heard. God save the Queen!' bellowed the tipstaff.

Mr Justice Cumquat looked fiercely at the jury. There definitely was something wrong with them. They sat there grinning like Cheshire cats, nudging one another, whispering behind their hands, giggling. He could not understand it.

Macquarie Q.C. now entered the fray in earnest. When he rose to make his closing address to the jury, it was a forensic *tour de force,* impassioned, cajoling, persuasive, eloquent, a display of brilliance, as he drove the last nails into Joe Tubb's coffin.

It was a very subdued Harry Pomfret who at length rose to follow him. He did his best, but his best was not good enough. Nothing he said could withstand Cumquat's onslaught as the Judge continually interrupted and badgered him, taunted and tormented him unmercifully. Still worse was the obvious fact that the jury were paying absolutely no attention to what he was saying.

When he finally sat down, with a heavy heart, Harry could

only think, 'We have lost . . . We have lost . . .' and he almost burst into tears. It was all so unfair.

Then Cumquat began his Charge to the jury. He had stayed up quite late preparing it, and every word was dipped in vitriol. 'The plaintiff says a gorilla threw the bananas which hit him on the head,' he told them, 'so he says . . .' And the jury was left in no doubt that His Honour was convinced that the plaintiff was a liar and a cheat.

He went on, 'But the defendant has called two witnesses, two completely independent witnesses, who do not know the plaintiff, and they say that no such thing occurred. If you believe those witnesses,' and again, there was no doubt His Honour did, 'if you believe those witnesses, members of the Jury, then the plaintiff must fail in this action.' By way of precaution, in case the action should ever go to the Court of Appeal, he added, 'Of course, it's a matter for you,' but in a tone of voice which implied that it was certainly not a matter for them, and they had better agree with what he said.

So he went on, systematically destroying the plaintiff's case, squeaking and smiling and smirking at the jury, charming them, leading them step by step to the complete undoing of Joe Tubb. By the time he was finished and the jury had retired to consider their verdict, young Pomfret was ashen-faced. Inexperienced as he was, he could hardly believe his ears, and kept wondering and wondering why the judge had so determinedly stuck his knife into the plaintiff.

Waiting for a jury to knock, to announce that they have arrived at a verdict, makes barristers nervous. Sometimes the jurors may go on arguing and shouting angrily at one another for hours on end, and the longer the barristers have to wait, the more nervous they become, hoping against hope, wondering and worrying. In order to encourage jurors to make up their minds quickly, it used to be the practice to lock them up for the night without food or drink, without fire or light. A cold winter's night was usually enough to spur those very hungry, shivering, thirsty, bleary-eyed 'good men and true' to announce a unanimous verdict the minute the Court convened the next morning. *Wretches hang that jurymen may dine,* scornfully wrote the poet Alexander Pope. Nowadays of course jurymen are fed — and at the State's expense, too — so there is less urgency, but not necessarily more logic, in their deliberations. In one case recorded in the Law Reports it appeared that a jury, after thirty hours' futile discussion, finally arrived at a decision by tossing a coin. And the arguments can go on for hours and hours as the tempers flare: it has been rumoured that one obstinate, quarrelsome Melbourne juror had his head held in the toilet by the other jurymen, and flushed and flushed and flushed, until he agreed to a unanimous verdict.

But in a civil case, such as an action for damages, Counsel for the plaintiff dreads a quick jury verdict, within 5 or 10 minutes, for this generally means that they have decided against his client. And in Joe Tubb's case, the jury had scarcely retired to their jury-room when they knocked.

'Well, that's it,' thought Pomfret, 'I've lost. — Unless,' he mused hopefully, giving St. Jude a quick rub, 'unless they want to ask a question . . . '

But the jury did not want to ask a question. They had indeed arrived at a verdict and were in a hurry to go off back to Maisie's place.

'Was there any negligence of King Kong or the Zoo which was a cause of the plaintiff's injuries?' asked the Judge's Associate.

'Yes,' replied the Foreman, to the chagrin and annoyance of the Judge.

'Was there contributory negligence on the part of the plaintiff?' asked the Judge's Associate.

'No,' replied the Foreman, to the even greater chagrin and annoyance of the Judge.

'At what sum do you assess the plaintiff's damages?' asked the Judge's Associate.

When he heard the indeed astronomical sum, Harry's jaw dropped in amazement, Macquarie Q.C. began to tremble like a leaf, and Mr Justice Cumquat fell backwards in his throne, his face a deathly pallor. The only person unaffected was Joe Tubb. But then, he was not listening. He was day-dreaming as to what horses he ought to back for the Trifecta on Saturday . . .

'Discharge the jury,' gasped Cumquat in a choking voice, and as the six of them filed out of Court, Harry turned around to watch them, his heart filled with joy and gratitude.

When she reached the door Maisie suddenly stopped, looked

back at Harry, glanced up at the Judge, again looked at Harry, smiled, and was gone.

Young Pomfret suddenly felt ten feet tall. Revenge tasted very sweet in his mouth. He stood, spreading his gown expansively about him. He gave a little pat of acknowledgement to St. Jude, pinned safely inside his Bar jacket, and, in a honeyed voice calculated precisely to rub salt into Cumquat's wound, he sweetly intoned, 'If Y'r Honour pleases, I move for judgment for the plaintiff . . . '

Cumquat did not reply.

Just as sweetly Harry repeated, 'If Y'r Honour pleases, I move for judgment for the plaintiff.'

Still Cumquat said nothing.

Once more Harry began, 'If Y'r Honour pleases—' but Macquarie had leant over and was tugging at the sleeve of his gown. Harry turned and regarded his learned friend in surprise.

In a voice filled with venom, Macquarie hissed, 'Eleven!'

For Mr Justice Cumquat had suffered a cardiac arrest. He was as dead as a doornail.

ENTER THE ATTORNEY-GENERAL

The death of Cumquat acted as a catalyst on an already tense situation: Two other Supreme Court judges immediately tendered their resignations. They had not yet reached the statutory retiring age of 72 years, but they had each notched up more than a decade on the Bench: This assured them of a pension for the rest of their life anyway, so they got out while the going was good.

Another younger judge, of less seniority, persuaded his doctor to admit him to the Mercy Hospital, for a prostate operation, which he had been putting off for years. To be on the safe side, and to keep himself well away from the hazards of judicial life, he decided to have another operation, for his haemorrhoids, while he was there, and even made tentative arrangements for a tonsillectomy, if things at the Law Courts did not improve.

A fourth, Mr Justice Smallbore, went overseas on Sabbatical leave. Supreme Court judges, like University professors, are entitled to an extended vacation every seven years. This is to enable them to make what is euphemistically described as an overseas study tour, and is supposed to blow any intellectual cobwebs out of their minds. Though, to be candid, the most exciting result of any such overseas tour that I can remember was when one of our Judges bought a ticket in the National Lottery in Rome, and won first prize.

The Chief Justice tried to persuade Smallbore not to take his Sabbatical leave at that crucial stage, not while the Supreme Court Bench was so alarmingly depleted. The Chief Justice pleaded and implored, he cajoled and bombasted, but Smallbore was adamant.

'If I don't go now, I may not live to get another chance,' he retorted. He was so determined, in fact, and so desperate, that he had even agreed to fly Garuda, that being the first available flight out of Melbourne.

And off he went to taste the flesh-pots of Paris, where he met a fille de joie in the Rue Saint-Jacques, accompanied her to a high-class bordel in Montparnasse, and was set upon by a group of voyous armed with matraques. His body, minus wallet, travellers' cheques and Diners' Club Card, was later fished out of the Seine near the Pont de Sèvres by the crew of a bateau-mouche. These sorry events were personally investigated by the Commissaire principal de police at the Quai des Orfèvres and have already been recorded by M. Georges Simenon in a slim volume entitled *Maigret et le Juge Mort de Melbourne.*

The Chief Justice called a meeting of the remaining members of the Bench to discuss the situation, but there were hardly enough of them to make a quorum—just himself, Sir George Philanderer, and a couple of other terrified Puisne Judges.

Meanwhile, there began to be murmurs in the City: Breaches of contract were not being litigated. The meanings of confused, illiterate home-made wills were not being judicially interpreted. Deeds of arrangement of insolvent companies with their debtors could not be approved. It was almost impossible to get a Writ of Habeas Corpus, a Mareva injunction or an Anton Piller order.

The Builders Labourers Federation, incensed that its members' claims for damages arising out of industrial accidents were not being tried, held noisy and violent demonstrations inside and outside the city offices of the major insurance companies, kicking in glass doors and emptying the contents of cupboards and desks all over the floors. The A.C.T.U. and the Trades Hall Council were threatening a general strike unless something was done soon.

Their cry was echoed by the newspapers. *Justice delayed is justice denied* declared an editorial of the *AGE*, with that Editor's usual startling originality. *COURT CHAOS CAUSES CATASTROPHE* screamed the front page of the *SUN*, while the publishers of the *HERALD* thundered *We demand of the Premier* . . .

Of course, the Council for Civil Liberties got into the act, and there was also an Ecumenical Service attended by the Catholic and Anglican Archbishops and other leading church dignitaries to pray for the State of Victoria and for a light to guide our civic leaders in these days of community distress. Unfortunately, the solemnity of this religious gabfest was somewhat marred by a spirited competition between the Salvation Army lassies and the shaven-headed saffron-robed devotees of Hare Krishna, the former banging their tambourines with rare abandon, crying 'Hallelujah! We want more judges! Hallelujah!', and the latter clanging their bells, beating their brass gongs, and stinking everyone out of the place with clouds of cheap Oriental incense which resembled closely the smell of burning dried cow-dung.

Prisoners at Pentridge gaol awaiting trial petitioned the Ombudsman. Question Time in the Legislative Assembly was in an uproar as Her Majesty's loyal Opposition banged their benches with their shoes and screamed, 'Shame! Shame!' Even the senior statesmen in the Legislative Council roused themselves temporarily from their terminal torpor to express gentle disquiet.

'Can't you recommend some names for us to appoint more judges?' the Premier phoned the Chief Justice.

'The barristers simply refuse to accept any appointments,' the poor man stuttered, 'They say the job is too dangerous.'

'Then the present judges will just have to work harder,' said the Premier.

The Chief Justice groaned. He was already reduced to hearing Orders Nisi to Review.

With the work of the Supreme Court practically brought to a standstill, many barristers' fee-books started to look very sick, a state of affairs which caused something of a cultural shock to the inhabitants of Barristers' Chambers. Questions began to be asked as to why the Senior Bar all refused elevation to the Bench, and soon word got around, with the help of Macquarie Q.C., that the Bar was nourishing a viper in its bosom—that for so long as Harry Pomfret remained on the scene, the judges would continue to be decimated, and no Counsel with any instinct for self-preservation would consent to a Supreme Court appointment.

So when one day I went with Harry to the Common Room for a mid-afternoon cup of coffee, our appearance caused a sudden, sullen hush, a move backwards as if we were a couple of lepers who had wandered in. Within a few minutes they had

A cultural shock

all left. 'I forgot to bring a bell to ring,' I snorted, as we sat there in glorious isolation.

'This state of affairs can't go on,' Sir George Philanderer was overheard to remark to the Chief Justice. 'If the Senior Bar won't accept elevation, we'll have to look elsewhere, lower down the ranks.'

'That would be most unconventional,' the Chief Justice protested unhappily, 'even irregular. The Supreme Court always looks to leaders of the Bar to fill any vacancies.'

Again, on a later occasion, Sir George was heard to express the very curious observation, 'If you can't beat them, you've got to join them, even if it means clutching the viper to our own bosom. My life is in danger and so is yours,' he went on, 'and we never know the day or the hour that he might strike again. As long as he has Dominic to hide behind, we are all at his mercy. Our very survival depends on putting him where we can keep on eye on him.'

'Oh dear, oh dear,' moaned the Chief Justice, 'I wish I knew what to do for the best.'

'Well if you take my advice,' Sir George Philanderer went on—but the door closed behind them, and what else was said we will never know.

It was during all this ferment that I received a message from the Attorney-General. Would I drop in to see him at his room at Parliament House? There was something he wanted to discuss with me.

So it had come to this, at last. With Macquarie and the rest of the Silks refusing appointments to the Bench, the Government was reduced to scraping the bottom of the barrel in its search for a judge. It was a kind gesture on the part of the Attorney-General, of course. We had known one another since our school days, when we had played cricket for our schools against one another. He had been a solicitor before he went into politics, and had sent me the occasional brief. But he knew, and I knew, that I was not really Supreme Court material. Perhaps ten years ago, when I was at my prime, I might have aspired to an appointment, but now it was too late, I was too old. Besides, to leave the companionship of the Bar and to exchange it for the isolation and loneliness of a judge's life would be too hard a wrench. I would have to refuse.

Then I thought of Amy, bless her. It would be a bitter disappointment for Amy, and the pension benefits of a judge might come in handy if she outlived me. But it was no use pretending I was something which I was not, and the more I thought about it the more convinced I became that I was just not good enough to be a Supreme Court judge.

So it was with a heavy heart that I climbed that long imposing flight of stairs that front the entrance to Parliament House. It is a grand building in the classical style, the portico supported by a row of great pillars and leading to the spacious Queen's Hall in the centre of which stands, high on a pedestal, a marble statue of Queen Victoria, with sceptre and orb and robed in all her regal and imperial 19th Century splendour.

'Take a chair, Dominic,' the Attorney-General said. 'There is a matter of some importance I wish to discuss with you.'

I sat down, but said nothing.

'As you no doubt know, the Government has been experiencing some difficulty in finding suitable appointments for the Supreme Court Bench, and the situation is causing us great embarrassment.'

I nodded, but did not comment.

'I have discussed the matter with the Chief Justice and the Senior Puisne Judge, and they have made a recommendation which I believe will help solve our problem.' He smiled encouragingly and went on, 'Of course we ordinarily would look to the Senior Bar for judicial appointments, but as they all refuse, we must look elsewhere, mustn't we?'

He was so charming, so obviously desperate to solve the Government's dilemma, that I began to wonder how I would have the heart to refuse him.

The Attorney-General took deep breath. 'Acting on the suggestion of the Chief Justice and Sir George Philanderer, I intend to advise the Governor-in-Council to appoint Mr Harry Pomfret a Justice of the Supreme Court of Victoria.'

I still said nothing—indeed I was bereft of speech! You could have, as they say, knocked me over with a feather. Completely thunderstruck, bewildered, unable to believe my ears, I gazed blankly at the Attorney-General.

'Of course I realize that Mr Pomfret is reading law with you, and as you are his Master I consider it appropriate to enquire whether you would release him from any commitments he may have made? And I would also appreciate any comments you may care to make, Dominic, on his suitability for such an appointment.'

The only remark that came to my mind was, 'But he's so young.'

'Yes, but William Pitt was Prime Minister of England at the age of 24. Age is not the only criterion. We have a crisis in the Law Courts and we have been led to believe that the elevation of Mr Pomfret to the Bench will solve it. So we intend to do just that, and be damned to the Senior Bar.'

I shook my head doubtfully.

'If we make this appointment, Dominic,' the Attorney-General went on, 'it will give the Silks such a shock that they will soon enough come to their senses. They will be down on their hands and knees begging us to choose them to fill the other vacancies on the Bench.' And he smiled cynically.

There was a long pause. My head was reeling at this extraordinary revelation, but gradually I began to collect my thoughts. There was no doubt in my mind that Harry would become a Supreme Court judge sooner or later. He was already determined on it and I didn't underestimate his driving ambition. So it might as well be sooner as later. Anyway, the appointment of a fresh young pup like that, instead of some old fogey of my vintage, might give a well-earned shake-up to the Bench. The words of William May, an Attorney-General of the early 1600's came to my mind: **Physicians, like beer, are best when they are old and stale, and lawyers, like bread, when they are young and new.** So, in for a penny, in for a pound—

'His age is a problem,' I mused as the Attorney-General listened attentively, 'but perhaps that could be overcome.'

'We can't wait until he's fifty or sixty, Dominic. We need him right now.'

'Yes,' I continued, 'but such a young Supreme court judge would need something to bolster his prestige, some little extra something. And I think you could give him that.'

'What have you in mind?' the Attorney-General asked, somewhat suspiciously, adding hurriedly, 'We couldn't pay him more than the other judges.'

'Nothing as drastic as that,' I smiled urbanely. 'But . . . but what about a knighthood? That would give him instant prestige and would cost you nothing.'

The Attorney-General's face was wreathed in smiles. 'An excellent idea,' he beamed. 'We could announce it with the Honours list for Queen's Birthday weekend.'

'That,' I nodded, with an ironic gleam in my eye, 'would be most appropriate.'

On the way back from Parliament House I called in at Judges' Chambers at the Supreme Court, and asked if Mr Justice Philanderer would see me. One of the Messengers went off to enquire, and returned with Philanderer's Associate. Yes, His Honour was in. Yes, he would see me. But His Honour was occupied at the moment, and would I care to wait? He wouldn't be long.

I glanced at my watch . . . George was probably drinking his afternoon cup of tea, I thought, so I would just have to kick my heels until he finished it.

'His Honour knows you're here,' the Associate said, and then he leant over and whispered conspiratorially, 'He's just finishing his cup of tea.' I have that sort of face: people always tell me things they should not.

Philanderer was still wearing his Court jacket, wing-collar and white bands when I entered his Chambers. He was smoking a cigar and waved me to an easy chair.

'What is it, Dominic?' he asked.

'I've just been to see the Attorney-General,' I replied.

'H'm . . . Well?'

'Harry's very young, George. Do you think he can handle the job?'

'We'll have to keep an eye on him at first, and give him some help. But he'll learn.'

There was a short embarrassed pause.

'George—' I began.

'Yes?'

'George, I once asked you if you were Harry's father . . . I'd like to ask you again. Are you?'

'No,' his answer was immediate and definite.

'I can't understand,' I said. 'You've been so unpleasant to him because of Clare, and now you recommend him for a Supreme Court appointment.'

'If you can't beat them, join them,' he answered tersely. 'Clare is determined to marry him, so I've just got to grin and bear it.'

'They are definitely not related?' I asked with some hesitation.

Philanderer looked at me curiously. 'What's eating you, Dominic?' he said, 'What's on your mind?'

'Young Pomfret tells me that his mother used to get cheques regularly from someone, but he doesn't know who. On at least one occasion a cheque came in an envelope marked *Judges' Chambers, Supreme Court, Melbourne.*'

'Well?'

'I've racked my brains again and again, and every time I come to the same conclusion: That the cheques were sent by you.'

Philanderer got up and went over to one of the tall windows of his Chambers. He stood there for a while, his back towards me, looking up at the sky. At length he replied, 'That's right. I sent those cheques.'

'But you just said you aren't his father.'

'That's right, Dominic,' he said, without turning around. 'I'm not his father.'

'Well, if you're not, who is?' I stood up in impatience.

Philanderer turned and came to me. He put his hand on my shoulder, gently eased me back into my chair, and said, 'You are.'

AMY, DEAR AMY

'Harry Pomfret was not conceived at the Pig and Whistle Hotel in the Blue Mountains,' George explained. 'He was conceived at the Pier Hotel at Frankston, and he was born at the Frankston Community Hospital.'

'But his mother told him he was conceived at the Pig and Whistle on Queen's Birthday weekend?'

'She was romancing. Do you remember that night when we got drunk at the Frankston Pier Hotel? And the two girls? My one's name was Marguerite. What was yours?'

'Beatrice,' I answered grimly. 'I thought they'd read those names in a book.'

'They did,' George replied. 'Those weren't their real names at all. Just more romancing. About eight months later I got a letter from one of the girls telling me she was going to have a baby and that I was the father. She said she had no money and would I send her some. So of course I did.' He paused. 'She wrote later that the baby had been born and would I send her some more money? I did. Then she said she needed money regularly. I had an allowance from my father, so I began to send her a cheque every week.' He fell silent.

'Yes?' I prompted.

'When I got engaged to be married, I decided to visit Harry's mother, to tell her that I wouldn't be able to send the money so often. But when I saw her, I realized that she was your girl, not mine.'

'Did she realize the mistake, too?'

'Yes,' George replied. 'The minute she saw me she knew she had the wrong man. But she said she didn't care which of us sent the money as long as one of us did, and every week.

Otherwise, she said, there'd be trouble, and as she had plenty of evidence that I'd been making regular payments for the baby, she'd say I was the father. I knew enough about law, even then, to know she had me over a barrel.'

There was a pause.

'What I don't understand, George,' I said, 'is that Harry is the dead spit of you when you were young.'

Philanderer gave a wry smile and walked over to a large mirror on the wall. 'Come here,' he called. I walked over and stood beside him.

'When we were at University,' he reminded me, 'they called us The Terrible Twins. Did you never think why? Look in the mirror.'

I looked. I was surprised. The same fair hair, now mostly grey, the same jaw, the same olive complexion, the same grey eyes . . . George was slightly taller, but otherwise we could have passed for brothers, not cousins.

'Have you never noticed the resemblance between Harry and Gerard?' Philanderer went on. 'They both look like you.'

'But Harry's mother told him his father was a judge,' I protested feebly.

'Romancing to the end,' George answered tersely. 'Besides, after receiving cheques from me year in and year out, she'd probably convinced herself by then that I really was his father.'

I was frankly stunned. Then a thought struck me. 'But that's shocking if you've been paying for my son all those years.'

'I sent the cheques,' George corrected me, 'but I didn't supply the money. Not after I discovered the truth, that is.'

'Well, who did provide the money?' I asked.

'You.'

'Oh no, George. I know that much.'

'Oh yes, Dominic. Every week for more than twenty years you paid for Harry Pomfret's keep and education.' I was about to protest but he went on. 'When I knew the truth, that I was not his father, I was going to tell you, but I wasn't quite sure how you would take it. So I told Amy.'

'You—told—AMY!'

'And she agreed that we shouldn't tell you. Amy said that a Christian Brothers education had left you with such a giant-sized guilt complex that if you really had something to feel guilty about, you'd be impossible to live with.'

'Amy said that???'

'Amy said that. And from then on, every week Amy put aside part of the housekeeping money you gave her, and sent it on to me and I wrote out a cheque and sent it to Harry's mother.'

'I had no idea . . .' I stammered.

'Of course not,' George agreed. 'You are just impractical, Dominic. You always have been. Who looks after all the money in your family? Amy! Who makes sure everything runs like clockwork for you? Amy! And when you lose your cases in Court, who tells you that it is not your fault at all, but that it was in the Stars, so don't get down-hearted?'

I shook my head in disbelief.

'The trouble with you, Dominic, is that you have never really appreciated what a gem of a wife Amy is. You just spend all your time belly-aching about how bad a cook she is, and you completely overlook her good points.'

I didn't reply. I couldn't. From what George had just told me, I had completely underestimated my wife, bless her, all through our married life. Unbeknown to me, it was Amy who had shouldered most of the burden . . . Like those pictures of the Holy Family—Joseph always carries a lily, while Mary carries the baby.

'When Gerard hurt his knee at football, while he was University,' George continued, 'Amy went to visit him. And there, right in the next bed, was Harry Pomfret. So, she got talking to him, liked him, and after he took his degree and wanted to read law at the Bar, guess who asked your clerk Arthur to persuade you to take him on?'

'Not Amy?'

'Amy. She made Arthur promise not to tell you though, in case you thought she was interfering. But she said to me that if the young man wanted to read law, then the proper place for him to do so was in his father's Chambers.'

'Does Harry know anything about all this, George?' I asked.

'No.'

'Well, don't tell him.'

'Why not?' he asked.

'Because he thinks his father is a Supreme Court judge. It may not be true, but it's a nice dream. If he ever discovers that his father is just an old also-ran hack barrister, he'd probably never forgive me.'

When I got home that evening, I found Amy in tears.

'What's wrong?' I asked anxiously.

'I burnt your dinner,' she wept.

I looked at her for a moment in amazement, then burst out laughing. 'For a quarter of a century you've ruined practically every meal I've eaten, and never once have you admitted that there was anything wrong with your cooking.' I continued to laugh, and kissed her. 'Come on, get your hat and coat, and I'll take you out for dinner to the most expensive restaurant in Melbourne.'

'We can't afford that, Dominic. We've got to put some money aside for when you retire.'

'I'll never retire,' I snorted. 'Come on, get your hat and coat.'

Well, it wasn't really the most expensive restaurant in Melbourne. In fact, it was only a little B.Y.O. place. Still . . .

'We got an invitation to a wedding today,' Amy told me.

'Anyone we know?'

'Clare Philanderer and that young man reading law with you.'

'That's nice,' I grunted.

'I'll wear my light grey dress with the pink buttons. I look nice in that.'

'I thought you were going to buy a new dress for their wedding?' I growled.

'It's all right, Dominic. We can't be wasting money like that.'

'I talked to George Philanderer for a long time today,' I said, and her eyes widened slightly, somewhat apprehensively. I took her hand across the table and held it for a minute before going on: 'What I mean to say is this, old girl: When my son marries, I want my wife to look a million dollars.'

And then, for some inexplicable reason, Amy burst into tears. She is a very difficult woman to understand, at times, bless her.

When she had at last settled down, and blown her nose on my handkerchief, she asked, 'It is all right, isn't it, Dominic? I mean, for Clare to marry Harry?'

'A man can't marry his grandfather's wife or his wife's son's daughter,' I replied, 'and a woman can't marry her husband's grandfather or her son's daughter's husband, but a man may

Just a little B.Y.O. place

marry his father's father's sister's son's daughter and a woman may marry her father's mother's brother's son's son.'

'Oh . . .' she said, somewhat doubtfully.

'My father was George Philanderer's mother's brother,' I explained, 'so Harry's grandfather's sister was Clare's grandmother. There's no impediment to the marriage.'

'Oh . . .' she repeated. 'Well, that's all right then.'

On the way home in the car, Amy said, 'Dominic, I have a confession to make.'

'Mm?' I was only half listening.

'Amelia Mutt came to see me today.'

'Mm?'

'She says she's pregnant.'

'That's nice,' I remarked. Then what Amy had just said hit me. 'Pregnant! That fool of a Gerard! I knew something like this would happen sooner or later! He's always chasing after girls! Now look what he's done!'

'Dominic,' Amy interrupted, very coolly, 'it wasn't Gerard.'

'Well,' I remarked, calming down, 'thank God for that.' Amy said nothing, but there was a world of meaning in her silence . . . 'Oh no,' I groaned. 'Not Harry?'

'Yes. Harry.'

'Well, he can't marry her. He's marrying Clare in two weeks time.'

'That's right,' Amy said, 'I've explained all that to Amelia.'

'What is she going to do?' I asked.

'I told her not to worry, that we'd adopt the baby.'

'Us!' I exploded 'You and me! Oh, come off it, Amy, we're too old for all that. Getting up at two o'clock in the morning to give the baby a bottle? At my time of life, I'd probably catch pneumonia. Besides, I've forgotten how to change a baby's nappy.'

'Then I'm afraid, Dominic, that you're just going to have to learn all over again. I promised Amelia that we would definitely adopt the baby, but only on condition that she never tells Harry he is the father. And it's all settled.'

I drove for a while in silence. History, according to Henry Ford, is bunk, but it certainly has a way of repeating itself. 'I hope,' I said at last, 'that this one is a girl. I'm sick of sons.'

'So am I, dear,' she agreed, and snuggled into my side.

As chance would have it, I was briefed to appear in the first case to be heard by His Honour Mr Justice Pomfret. I glanced through the papers in my brief, and was overjoyed to see that at last someone had sent me a brief which was an open and shut case, completely foolproof. There was absolutely no way I could lose, because otherwise I would have refused to accept the brief. I mean, it would look bad, wouldn't it, if at his very first trial His Honour had to deliver judgment against the Counsel who only last week had been his Master? Let alone his own father!

My cup of joy overflowed when I found that my opponent in the action was none other than Macquarie Q.C. That learned Silk was thunderstruck when he heard of Harry's appointment. Once he had recovered his wits, he sent out discreet semaphore messages to the Attorney-General, letting him know gently that yes, Macquarie Q.C. had now changed his mind and would graciously accept elevation to the Bench. Not so discreet semaphore messages came back, loud and clear, that the Attorney-General had not the slightest intention of inviting Macquarie Q.C. to sit on the Supreme Court Bench, not now, not ever. Political grudges last a long while.

So now Macquarie had to appear before Mr Justice Pomfret, had to bow to Mr Justice Pomfret, had to say 'Yes, Y'r Honour . . . No, Y'r Honour . . .' And what's more, he was in the first case to be heard by His Honour and he held a lousy brief which was a dead-set loser. A very bitter pill for Macquarie Q.C.

Amy was delighted. 'I'd like to come and watch,' she said, 'but I'm sure I'd clap or cheer when Harry finds in favour of your client. Your Stars have taken quite a turn for the better, Dominic. It says in the morning paper that all your ventures this week will be successful and come to happy fruition.'

Of course, just to be on the safe side, as I entered the courtroom I rubbed my own St Jude medal, for good luck.

Unfortunately—

Still, we can't win them all, can we?

POSTSCRIPT

If you are still wondering who blew up the Opscotch yacht, burned down the Pig and Whistle, shipped Harry off to Saudi Arabia—and whether Amelia Mutt's baby was a boy or a girl . . .

Well, I'm afraid you'll just have to wait for the sequel.